Proclaiming the Resurrection

PROCLAIMING THE RESURRECTION

Papers from the First Oak Hill College
Annual School of Theology

Edited by
Peter M. Head

paternoster
press

First published 1998 by Paternoster Press

04 03 02 01 00 99 98   7 6 5 4 3 2 1

Paternoster Press is an imprint of Paternoster Publishing,
P.O. Box 300, Carlisle, Cumbria, CA3 0QS, U.K.
http: //www.paternoster-publishing.com

British Library Cataloguing in Publication Data
A catalogue record for this book is available from the British Library.

ISBN 0-85364-824-7

This book is printed using Suffolk New Book paper which is 100% acid free.

Cover design by Mainstream, Lancaster
Typeset by Design2Print, Droitwich, Worcs.
Printed in Great Britain by Clays Ltd., Bungay, Suffolk

Contents

Abbreviations

BAGD	W. Bauer, W.F. Arndt, F.W. Ginrich and F.W. Danker, *Greek-English Lexicon of the NT*
BST	*The Bible Speaks Today*
ET	*Expository Times*
ICC	International Critical Commentary
IDB	*Interpreter's Dictionary of the Bible*
JSNTSS	*Journal for the Study of the New Testament Supplement Series*
JSOT	*Journal for the Study of the Old Testament*
NCBC	New Century Bible Commentary
NEB	New English Bible
NICNT	New International Commentary on the New Testament
NICOT	New International Commentary on the Old Testament
NIV	New International Version
OTL	Old Testament Library
REB	Revised English Version
RSV	Revised Standard Version
SBEC	Studies in the Bible and Early Christianity
SBLMS	Society of Biblical Literature Monograph Series
SNTSMS	Society for New Testament Studies Monograph Series
TDNT	*Theological Dictionary of the New Testament*, ed. G. Kittel and G. Friedrich
TOTC	Tyndale Old Testament Commentary
WBC	World Biblical Commentary
WUNT	Wissenschaftliche Untersuchungen zum Neuen Testament

Introduction

The resurrection of Jesus Christ from the dead is the foundation upon which any contemporary expression of Christian faith must take its stand. Any contemporary expression, that is, which could claim continuity with the historic faith of the apostolic church. In Paul's words, 'If Christ has not been raised, your faith is futile and you are still in your sins' (1 Cor. 15:17). It is this conviction which explains the right and proper concern among most Christians, and particularly among evangelical and conservative Christians, to defend the historicity of the physical/bodily resurrection of Jesus against sceptics of all sorts. But if the significance of Jesus' resurrection is construed merely in terms of it having happened, aspects of the significance of the resurrection for Christian faith and life can lie undiscovered in the pages of the New Testament, and the church's witness to the risen Lord may be weakened. Jesus Christ's victory over death and sin, his elevated status as Lord, the coming of the Spirit, the blessings of salvation and the sure hope of eternal life are among a host of theological truths which are all dependent upon the resurrection and need to be explored and appreciated in its light.

It was with a view to exploring some aspects of the theological importance and pastoral relevance of the resurrection of Jesus Christ that the faculty of Oak Hill College organized our first Annual School of Theology, on 16 April 1997, and presented the papers now published in this collection. The School of Theology had two aims, both of which are reflected in this book. First, and foremost, the day was envisaged as the climax of a process of scholarly activity involving individual reflection and mutual and interdisciplinary thinking on the subject of Jesus' resurrection. Initial versions of the papers were read, discussed and debated at a series of staff meetings leading up to the presentation of the papers to the public. This whole process is an ongoing one, as the 'Annual' makes clear, with the aim of stimulating staff development, individually and as a team, whose teaching ministries within the college are further complemented by a wider ministry of helpful, relevant and clear biblical and theological writing on matters of contemporary or universal importance.

The second aim for the School of Theology revolved around the public presentation of the papers in such a way that would contribute to the encouragement and stimulation of our former students, other clergy and Christian workers. A few words about the day itself may give readers a feel for the event and help to place the essays which follow into their appropriate context. Over 150 people booked in for the School, almost entirely Christian workers from London and the South-East of England. The lectures took place in the college chapel, the only room big enough to contain the crowd! This setting, combined with the singing of resurrection hymns at the beginning and close of the morning and afternoon sessions, contributed to the feeling that solid theological thinking could hold hands with heartfelt praise and worship. The biblical papers were presented in the morning, and after an excellent lunch the historical and theological papers in the afternoon. Special thanks are due to Peter Wood for his smooth management of all the practical matters relating to the day.

It is hoped that the publication of these essays may stimulate and encourage a wider readership in their thinking and reflection about *Proclaiming the Resurrection*. There are already a large number of books on the resurrection, including several recent collaborative efforts, such as the 1993 volume of *Ex Auditu* (Chicago: North Park Symposium); and four recent books: Paul Avis (ed.), *The Resurrection of Jesus Christ* (London: Darton, Longman & Todd, 1993); Stephen Barton and Graham Stanton (eds.), *Resurrection: Essays in Honour of Leslie Houlden* (London: SPCK, 1994); Gavin D'Costa, *Resurrection Reconsidered* (Oxford: Oneworld, 1996); Stephen T. Davis, Daniel Kendall & Gerald O'Collins (eds.), *The Resurrection: An Interdisciplinary Symposium on the Resurrection of Jesus* (Oxford: OUP, 1997). While this itself proves the contemporary vitality of reflection on the subject, it also demands some justification for adding another book to the flood. What contribution does this collection make that the others have not?

The answer to this is both collective and individual. Clearly the contributors reflect a more consistently evangelical and conservative approach to the subject than any of the other collections just mentioned. We have refrained from addressing the resurrection of Jesus primarily as a historical question, believing both that this task has been done often enough by conservatives and that by addressing the various biblical-theological questions we might make a distinctive contribution to contemporary evangelical thinking on the resurrection of Jesus.[1] We have obviously not been able to offer anything like a comprehensive study of the resurrection of Jesus in all of its many facets, but by probing a number of crucial issues we have made a coherent contribution to the literature.

The contributions of the individual papers are more simple to elucidate. The first chapter seeks to address the problem raised by the repeated New Testament insistence that Jesus' resurrection was 'according to the Scriptures' (1 Cor. 15:3f; cf. Lk. 24:22–27; Jn. 20:3-9). What can be said about this from the perspective of the Old Testament itself in which resurrection can hardly be said to make a dominant impact on Israel's faith and life? What sort of antecedents to Jesus' resurrection, whether individual, national, or messianic, are found there? Mike Butterworth is well qualified to address these questions, having taught Old Testament at Oak Hill for fifteen years, and having honed his exegetical skills in his work on *Structure and the Book of Zechariah* (Sheffield: Sheffield Academic, 1992). Mike's wide-ranging and straightforwardly honest approach makes a clear contribution to our understanding of the Old Testament hope of resurrection. He has recently become Principal of the St Albans and Oxford Ministry Training Scheme.

---

[1] Contributions defending the historicity of Jesus' resurrection can be found in a number of the other collections mentioned above. Other influential works include G.E. Ladd, *I Believe in the Resurrection of Jesus* (Grand Rapids: Eerdmans, 1975); W.L. Craig, *Assessing the New Testament Evidence for the Historicity for the Resurrection of Jesus* (SBEC 16; Lewiston/Queenston/ Lampeter: Edwin Mellen, 1989); M.J. Harris, *From Grave to Glory: Resurrection in the New Testament* (Grand Rapids: Zondervan, 1990).

Both of the New Testament papers reflect explicitly on the Old Testament background of resurrection faith and its impact on the two most voluminous of the New Testament writers. The first of these, dealing with Luke–Acts, explores the Lukan emphases on the Scriptural predictions and the physical reality of Jesus' resurrection. Beginning from Luke 24, David Peterson explores the role played by the resurrection of Jesus in the preaching and apologetic of the early apostles. Particular attention is paid to the use of the OT in Peter's Pentecost sermon in Acts 2. The paper concludes with some reflections on the impact of Luke's presentation on Jewish and Gentile audiences and its relevance for contemporary apologetics. David Peterson has been Principal of Oak Hill College since September 1996. His exegetical interests have been focused on Acts for some years and along with his work on *Witness to the Gospel* (Grand Rapids & Cambridge: Eerdmans, 1998), a collection of essays on the theology of Acts which he has edited with I.H. Marshall, this essay represents some of the first-fruits of that interest.

The third chapter attempts to deal with Paul's view of the resurrection by focusing on his letter to the Romans. Essentially the argument is that Paul's understanding of the resurrection of Jesus as the key to his messianic Lordship over the nations is derived primarily from reflection on various OT passages. This explains both its centrality to the argument and appeal of Romans and the otherwise un-Pauline emphasis on the Davidic descent of Jesus in Romans. For Paul, the faith, life and hope of a Christian are all conceived as fundamentally resurrection-centred. This paper, really only a brief summary of the wealth of material that could be addressed from Romans, grew out of my own regular opportunities to teach the epistle to Romans to keen third-year students at Oak Hill College. It also relates tangentially to my ongoing interest in the influence of the OT on the christological reflection of the NT writers (cf. on a different tack my *Christology and the Synoptic Problem* (Cambridge: CUP, 1997)).

With the fourth and fifth chapters we move from biblical studies to historical and theological studies. Rudi Heinze deals with a very neglected aspect of Puritan thought. Drawing upon the works of four Puritans (William Perkins, Thomas Goodwin, Stephen Charnock and Thomas Manton) he traces the impact of the biblical witness on their life and thought. Particular attention is drawn to their diverse beliefs about which person in the godhead had the major role in the resurrection of Jesus. By showing the way in which the resurrection of Jesus functioned as a prime source of comfort and reassurance to the believer, Heinze offers an important corrective to a number of recent studies which have emphasized the problems of doubt and despair which some Puritans experienced. Rudi Heinze has taught Church History at Oak Hill College for almost twenty years and retired at the beginning of 1998. His teaching, enthusiasm, godliness and pastoral care will be sorely missed. His publications, covering the whole field of Christian history since the reformation, are too numerous to list, but include *The Proclamations of the Tudor Kings* (Cambridge: CUP, 1977) and *Dedham and the Puritans* (Dedham Lecture, 1994).

Whereas evangelical theology has always been at home among the Puritans, it has not always known exactly what to do with the massive legacy of Karl Barth. Martin Davie argues that evangelicals must face the challenge of an ongoing critical dialogue with Barth. Davie argues that although Barth affirms both the bodily nature of Jesus' resurrection and the historicity of the empty tomb tradition, his interests are in the theological significance of the resurrection in a number of areas, both theological and pastoral. Having discussed these areas Davie responds to Barth's scepticism about the actual resurrection narrative and offers six lessons which must be learnt from Barth. Martin Davie teaches both Christian Doctrine and Church History at Oak Hill College. His Oxford D Phil has been published as *British Quaker Theology since 1895* (Lewiston: Edwin Mellen, 1997).

Careful readers will no doubt observe differences of style, emphasis and even content among the different writers.[2] It is hoped that as a whole they will encourage those charged with proclaiming the resurrection, by stimulating thought on the theological significance of the resurrection for Jesus, for his followers, and for the world. We have asked each contributor to facilitate this ongoing process by including some 'Questions for

---

[2] The editor would like to thank Iain Taylor for his careful proof-reading of the manuscript.

Reflection' and listing a few key books or articles after each paper. Doubtless a great deal more could and will be said on the subject, just as some of our papers are clearly preliminary findings in need of further careful exegetical and theological reflection. It is hoped that these papers reflect something of Oak Hill's commitment to a robust evangelical theology in dialogue with the wider scholarly community, but nourished by and permanently attuned to the teaching of Holy Scripture.

Peter M. Head (editor)

One

Old Testament Antecedents to Jesus' Resurrection

MIKE BUTTERWORTH

1. Introduction and General Considerations

There seems to be evidence from all over the world, at all times in history, and from very unsophisticated people today (especially children), that questions and answers about life after death come fairly naturally to human beings. This has a bearing on the presuppositions with which we approach the Old Testament, because one of the puzzling questions that arises from a study of the Old Testament is, 'Why is there so little interest in life after death in the OT and why are there even texts that appear to deny any possibility that there is such a thing?'[1] Israel's lack of interest needs explanation, so atypical is it in the context of ancient religions. Even in Mesopotamia, where

---

[1] G. von Rad comments: 'The realm of the dead remained an indefinable third party between Yahweh and his creation. Apart from isolated questionings (e.g. Job 14:13-22), it was not a subject of real interest to faith. Poetic fancy alone took it up now and then (Isa. 14:9ff.; Ezek. 32:20ff.). Should we not see this theological vacuum, which Israel zealously kept free from any sacral concepts . . . as one of the greatest theological enigmas in the Old Testament?' (*Old Testament Theology* (Edinburgh: Oliver & Boyd, 1965), vol. 2, 350).

immortality was thought to be generally unattainable, the Gilgamesh Epic gives great attention to the subject.[2]

It is noticeable in reading commentaries on the texts discussed below that the conclusion can usually be guessed from the theological position of the commentator. No doubt my own conclusions will also be predictable. In general, commentators of a 'liberal' frame of mind, who tend not to believe that Christ was literally raised from the dead, also doubt that life after death (in any form) is taught in the Old Testament. They tend to argue along the following lines: there is very little that could be thought to teach life after death; some texts actually deny that there is life after death; the texts that seem to teach life after death all contain uncertainties, and, therefore, these texts should probably be interpreted in some other way.

The normal traditional and conservative approach has tended to be structured along rather different lines. For example: the Bible as a whole clearly teaches life after death for the individual; the Old Testament must be in harmony with this view, and therefore, it is likely that the texts which seem to teach life after death really do so; and, those texts which seem to deny life after death must be interpreted in some other way.

In this essay I shall begin with an investigation of Old Testament conceptions of death and what follows it (section II). I shall argue that the Old Testament does imply some sort of continued existence of the individual after death, and that even without the New Testament we should have to conclude that there is a relationship with God that continues after death. I shall then consider a selection of those texts that have traditionally been thought to teach life after death. The first group of texts (section III) will be those referring to a general resurrection (life after death for people in general). I start with the most certain (Dan. 12:2f) and then deal with the other three

---

[2] The Gilgamesh Epic dates from c. 2600 BC and deals with the adventures of Gilgamesh, king of Uruk in Southern Mesopotamia. Similar versions of the story or parts thereof have been found from different dates and places within the same general region. It contains the story of how Utnapishtim obtained eternal life, but teaches that this is a unique attainment, not open to Gilgamesh or any other mortal. See J.M. Sasson, 'Gilgamesh Epic' in *The Anchor Bible Dictionary* (6 vols.; ed. D.N. Freedman; New York, et al.: Doubleday, 1992), vol. 2, 1024–7, for a convenient summary; or in more detail, A. Heidel, *The Gilgamesh Epic and Old Testament Parallels* (Chicago: University of Chicago Press, 1946).

in the order in which they occur in the Hebrew Bible: Isaiah 26:19; Psalm 49; Job 19:25–7. I shall then consider a text relating to the resurrection of the Messiah: Isaiah 52:13-53:12, and a briefer discussion of two other texts: Psalms 16:9–11 and 17:15 (section IV). With respect to all these texts we shall have to examine the reasons which have been advanced for doubting their applicability to the subject in hand, and then attempt to establish first, the minimum implication with respect to life after death; and second, the most likely meaning of the text in question.

If scholars disagree about the witness of the Old Testament to life after death in any form (as they certainly do) there are still a number of propositions that are generally agreed. I summarize them as follows, as they provide a useful starting point for our investigation:

1. The Old Testament does not say very much about life after death. The focus is clearly on life in this world.

2. Some texts seem to rule out life after death completely, or at least imply that the author did not have any hope of life after death.

3. A few texts, of which detailed and precise exegesis is uncertain, could be understood as teaching life after death for the individual.

4. One text definitely teaches the resurrection of at least some people, both good and bad.

2. Old Testament conceptions of death and afterwards

There is very little about life after death in the Old Testament

The focus of most of the Old Testament is firmly on *this life*. The terms of God's covenant with Israel, involving the enjoyment of God's blessing *in the land*, actually encouraged this. If a person dies, then usually that's that. There's a sort of satisfaction in dying 'in a good old age' or 'full of years.'[3] But we note also several facts that have a bearing on the underlying conception of the Israelites' faith.

First of all, contact with the dead was forbidden. It is not said that it is impossible. The possible success of necromancers is not pronounced upon. Deuteronomy 18:10f. says, 'There shall not be found among you anyone who practises divination . . . or a necromancer (literally 'a seeker to the dead'). We cannot be absolutely sure whether the medium of Endor did or did not contact the real Samuel. The writer certainly does not deny that the dead are somewhere to be contacted. Similarly we note that in Isaiah 8:19 the prophet condemns with the rhetorical question those who consult mediums, 'Should not a people consult their God? Should they consult the dead on behalf of the living?'

This is consistent with the fact that many texts refer to places in the universe other than the earth. Most obviously God is 'in heaven' or in 'his holy place/sanctuary.' So, although one might acknowledge that nothing is outside of God's influence and that 'heaven and the highest heaven cannot contain' him (1 Kgs. 8:27) they can still pray 'O Lord, hear in heaven your dwelling place, and when you hear, forgive'(vv. 30, 34, 39, 43, 45, 49). There are similar prayers elsewhere, for example, '[O Lord] look down from heaven' (Isa. 63:15; and Bar. 2:16 also). In fact there are scores of examples in which it is stated or implied that the Lord is in heaven (starting with Gen. 21:17 and 22:11 where God called to Hagar and Abraham respectively from heaven), or in

---

[3] At least there is satisfaction to someone who didn't believe they had the right or the possibility of living a long life. Perhaps the interest in life after death in later Judaism is due to rising expectations. Philip Johnston argues that Sheol is viewed negatively: it is the place for which the wicked are destined, but which the righteous expect or hope to escape. He notes the contrast between Jacob in Gen. 37:35 (cf. 42:38 and 44:29, 31), feeling depressed and expecting to 'go down to Sheol mourning', and the way his actual (contented) death is described: 'dies; sleeps with his father; breathes his last; is gathered to his people' (see 46:30; 47:29f.; 48:21; 49:29, 33; 50:5, 16, 24, 26). Note that Jacob does say 'go down to my son to Sheol', presumably indicating the place to which even a good son goes if 'an evil beast hath devoured him!' (37:20, 33 AV). See his 'Left in Hell? Psalm 16, Sheol and the Holy One' in P.E. Satterthwaite, R.S. Hess, and G.J. Wenham (eds.), *The Lord's Anointed: Interpretation of Old Testament Messianic Texts* (Carlisle: Paternoster, 1995), 213–22, esp. 219.

his own dwelling place (cf. Hos. 5:15, 'I will return to my place . . .').[4]

Along with this fact we note two well-known, but nevertheless remarkable, passages: Genesis 5:24, 'Enoch walked with God, and he was not, for God took him' – or we might translate, 'God received him.' The phrase 'he was not' is one word in Hebrew (one word with a personal suffix): 'non-existence of him', but not in a sort of philosophical sense of absolute non-existence. Rather it's 'he wasn't there' (any more). We will not dwell on this text since scholars seem to agree that it means God took Enoch to be with him.

Similarly 2 Kings 2:11, 'And Elijah went up by a whirlwind into heaven.' The story is told how Elisha's companions rather doubted that he had gone into heaven and sent out a search party to see if the Lord had deposited him on a mountain or in a valley somewhere. Elisha permitted them to go, although he was embarrassed by their lack of faith (v. 18).

So it is admitted that the earth is not the only place in the universe. There is also heaven and there is also Sheol.[5] Many times it occurs simply as a way of saying that someone dies, and it is often used in parallel with 'the pit' and 'the grave.' But it is clear that many times it is thought of as an actual place. For example, Genesis 37:35, [Jacob says] 'No, I shall go down to Sheol to my son, mourning'; in Numbers 16:30 we read; 'But if the Lord creates something new, and the ground opens its mouth, and swallows them up, with all that belongs to them, and they go down *alive* into Sheol, then you shall know that these men have despised the Lord' (My italics, obviously).

We note also the temporary resurrections (or more properly resuscitations); 1 Kings 17:17–24; 2 Kings 4:18–37; 13:20–21, although we cannot base very much upon these narratives. Similarly, I do not think we can prove anything significant from Ezekiel 37:1–14, the valley of dry bones. The vision concerns

---

[4] See also Pss. 73:25f.; 139:7f.; 144:7; 150:1, etc.

[5] In a long discussion of 'descent to the underworld' R. Bauckham shows that the Old Testament contains little of this in comparison with other nations of the ancient world. The theory that Ps. 24:7–10 is a remnant of a myth in which a high god (identified as Yahweh in the Psalm) goes down to Sheol to confront the powers of death is rejected by Bauckham; 'Descent to the Underworld', *Anchor Bible Dictionary*, vol. 2, 145–59.

individuals but the meaning is that the nation of Israel will be restored. The original meaning of v. 12, 'I will open your graves, and raise you from your graves . . .' is clearly metaphorical.[6]

Some texts imply either that there is no life after death or that the author did not have any hope of life after death

There are several, but a sample of some of the most forceful would include:

2 Samuel 14:14 [The woman of Tekoa said] 'We must all die, we are like water spilt on the ground, which cannot be gathered up again . . .'

Psalm 6:5, For in death there is no remembrance of you; in Sheol who can give you praise?

Psalm 30:8, To you, O Lord, I cried; and to the Lord I made supplication: 9. 'What profit is there in my death, if I go down to the Pit? Will the dust praise you? Will it tell of your faithfulness?'

Psalm 88:2, Let my prayer come before you . . . 4. I am reckoned among those who go down to the Pit; I am a man who has no strength, 5. like one forsaken among the dead, like the slain that lie in the grave, like those whom you remember no more, for they are cut off from your hand . . . 10. Do you work wonders for the dead? Do the shades rise up to praise you? 11. Is your steadfast love declared in the grave, or your faithfulness in Abaddon? 12. Are your wonders known in the darkness, or your saving help in the land of forgetfulness? (The answer expected is clearly 'No'.)

Isaiah 38:10, I said, 'In the noontide of my days I must depart; I am consigned to the gates of Sheol for the rest of my years.' 11. I said, 'I shall not see the Lord in the land of the living; I shall look upon man no more among the inhabitants of the world . . .' 18. For Sheol cannot thank you, death cannot praise you; those who go down to the pit cannot hope for your faithfulness.

We might offer at least two responses to statements like these. One is that they express the views of particular speakers and

---

[6] Although one might call this a 'conjuring trick with bones', it is more in line with Hebrew thought than the doctrine of the immortality of the soul which developed during the inter-testamental period, e.g. Wis. Sol. 7–8.

these views may or may not be right. Even the prophets did not know everything and may have made mistakes when not reporting the word of the Lord. I expect Isaiah bought his wife the occasional unwanted gift. It is also true that words may be used figuratively or poetically or incidentally, and should not be made the basis for a hard doctrine. So in Psalm 88 it seems clear that the Psalmist does *not* believe that he will be in God's presence if he actually dies. We, however, as post-resurrection Christians, believe that he would have been.

The problem with this response is made acute, however, by the fact that the Psalms were authorized to be said or sung by the congregation. So it is not just a question of 'people expressing their own thoughts.' They are authorized to pray these things. For the Christian this is comparable (but not identical) to the problem caused by the imprecatory psalms, those psalms in which the speaker curses his or her enemy (e.g. Ps. 109:6–20 is a fairly comprehensive prayer, quoted with reference to Judas in Mt. 27:39; Mk. 15:29) rather than 'turning the other cheek' or 'blessing those that curse him.'[7] It seems to me that it is necessary for us to maintain distance as well as identification when saying both the imprecatory psalms and those that seem to deny life after death. In other words, I sing someone else's song, allowing that there are resonances with my own experience.[8] In dealing with the imprecatory psalms as 'a problem' we note, in passing, also their positive implications: 'It is OK to feel this way and to express these feelings to God. It is OK if you lack assurance. You're not the first to feel this way. Just hang on to God, because he *is* there.'

The other response to interpreting the texts is to point out that from the point of view of observers on earth, dead people do not praise the Lord, in fact they don't do anything. They do not return to life. So if we take a 'geocentric' interpretation most

---

[7] Even if Psalm 109:6–19 is taken to be a quotation of words spoken by the enemy, the psalmist still prays in v. 20 for the same to be visited upon him. Further see John Shepherd, 'The Place of the Imprecatory Psalms in the Canon of Scripture', *Churchman* 111 (1997), 27–47 ('Part One'), and 110–26 ('Part Two'); originally his Honours Dissertation, Oak Hill College, 1996.

[8] Presumably this was the same for the Israelites of old. The book of Job is a good example of a biblical writing which displays a subtle view of the way in which truth can be expressed, cf. for example, Job 42:3, 7.

texts which could be used to deny belief in any sort of afterlife are simply empirical statements concerning the difference between a dead body and a living person.[9]

Philip Johnston offers a new and radical way of interpreting texts relating to death. He notes that the individuals who are presumed to be righteous but who envisage descent to Sheol all speak in the context of extreme trial (loss, illness, affliction or abandonment) or of divine judgment.[10]

Either way the Christian who believes that the Bible should interpret itself, must read these texts (as all texts) in the context of the whole Bible. To summarize: the Israelites were not completely unaware of questions relating to life after death. They were strongly encouraged to focus on this life, but they had some sort of awareness of life elsewhere. Their world-view allowed for a later development of life after death.

3. Texts Relating to a General Resurrection or Life After Death

Daniel 12:2

The one passage of the Old Testament that everyone believes teaches the resurrection of the individual to eternal life or judgment is Daniel 12:2. Despite this T.H. Gaster says that 'this passage does not represent a natural development of previous Hebrew thinking, but is simply a clever exploitation of popular "pagan" notions, designed . . . to reassure the devout, and . . . to

---

[9] Willem A. VanGemeren believes that verses such as we have been considering do not indicate 'that the OT denies life after death, but rather it puts the emphasis on the present life as the most important stage in man's relationship with God. The Psalmist believes that there is *still* life to live and that there is therefore still time to praise the Creator!', 'Psalms', *The Expositor's Bible Commentary* (Grand Rapids: Zondervan, 1991), vol. 5, 99; see also 569–73.

[10] 'Left in Hell?', 219 (see n. 3 above), referring also to R. Rosenberg, *The Concept of Biblical Sheol within the Context of Ancient Near Eastern Beliefs* (PhD, Harvard University, 1981), 88. Johnston's own dissertation argues this position more fully, see Philip S. Johnston, *The Underworld and the Dead in the Old Testament*, (PhD, Cambridge University, 1993), which I have unfortunately not been able to consult.

hoist infidels with the petard of their own apostatic [i.e. apostate] beliefs.'[11]

This passage comes at the climax of a long and intricate chapter about events beginning in the Greek Period (second century BC), which describes a conflict between kings in Persia and Greece. Daniel 12:1 reads, 'At that time shall arise Michael, the great prince who has charge of your people . . . and there shall be a time of trouble . . . but at that time your people shall be delivered, every one whose name is found written in the book.' There are difficulties in interpreting the details of ch. 11, but all agree that this culmination is an eschatological prophecy: it deals with the last and completely decisive action of God in human history. What is not agreed is the date of this passage. Most 'liberal' scholars regard it as belonging to the second century, while most conservative commentators favour the sixth century, the period in which the narratives found in Daniel are set. John Goldingay was the first conservative commentator, as far as I can tell, to argue for a second century date for Daniel.[12]

The issue is important for it affects the interpretation of other texts which provide less certain evidence of belief in the resurrection of the individual. If the doctrine of individual resurrection only arose in this late period, then it is improbable that we have any earlier references to it, and apparent references will need to be interpreted in some other way. The relevance of Gaster's argument for my own investigation is that, *if* he is right, then Daniel 12 cannot be used to argue that *other texts* are likely to anticipate belief in the resurrection of the dead. I believe that I have shown above that the Old Testament is wholly consistent with belief in life after death, and therefore the presence of this doctrine in Daniel 12 cannot be called unnatural.[13]

We note also that all commentators, including Gaster, agree

---

[11] Gaster, 'Resurrection' in *Interpreter's Dictionary of the Bible* (Nashville: Abingdon, 1962), vol. 4, 39–43, quotation from 39f.

[12] J.E. Goldingay, *Daniel* (WBC; Waco: Word, 1987). Some would say that this disqualifies him from being called conservative, since it's more than a 10 per cent swing to liberal. Apologies to readers who are now further away from the British general election than when these frivolous words were uttered.

[13] See further, J.J. Collins, *Daniel with an Introduction to Apocalyptic Literature* (Grand Rapids: Eerdmans, 1984), 103. He argues that there was no change in theology through Dan. 8–12, and that chs. 7 and 12 are complementary.

that there *was* a doctrine of individual resurrection in place at least by the second century before Christ. This doctrine was a double resurrection: the wicked as well as the righteous are raised from 'the dust of the earth', i.e. their graves, and are consigned to everlasting shame and contempt. An unusual feature of the text is that it seems to envisage the resurrection as taking place at the same time as a great distress. The easiest way of interpreting this is to assume that the resurrection brings this time to an end. We can hardly assume that the righteous dead awake to a time of tribulation when the context seems to speak of a final sorting out of good and evil. Despite this general agreement, there are several features of the text that require a more detailed discussion:

At that time: This common expression is often used fairly loosely and it is difficult to pinpoint its exact reference. It follows the account of the king who will act as he pleases. Commentators have generally agreed that this refers in the first instance to Antiochus Epiphanes (Antiochus IV, 175–163 BC, the Seleucid ruler whose empire included Palestine). Conservative commentators usually argue that it *also* refers to an eschatological figure who is described in the New Testament as the Antichrist. In other words, there is a dispute about whether the reference is primarily or exclusively to the second century BC. Those who restrict the meaning to Antiochus usually also believe that the writer wrongly assumed that the end time would follow immediately. For our purposes, therefore, we may assume that the context for 12:1ff. is the last times. This is confirmed in 11:40, *at the time of the end*, which is the last time indication before 12:1.

Many: This gives the impression in English that not all will be resurrected, and this would suggest a conception that would be difficult to fit into a biblical view of the end times (heaven – hell – continuing 'sleep'). The force of the usage in Hebrew seems to be 'multitudes' as Joyce Baldwin helpfully points out, noting a number of passages in which 'many' (*rabbim*) occurs; e.g. Deuteronomy 7:1 ('when the Lord clears away many nations before you'); Isaiah 2:2–3 ('all nations' is parallel to 'many peoples'); Isaiah 52:14f.; 53:11f. ('many' has inclusive force).[14]

However, this does not entirely solve the problem since the expression used is 'Many *from* those who sleep in the dust of the earth . . .' and this does suggest that there are some who do not wake up. Interpretations of this include the following:

1. The writer focuses on those who died in the great battle(s) mentioned in ch. 11. Those on the side of good are raised to everlasting life, those who opposed them are raised to shame/reproach and everlasting contempt/abhorrence (only found elsewhere in Isa. 66:24, in a similar context).

2. The language should not be pressed to this extent: the writer is not considering the question whether some or all of the dead are raised, but drawing attention to the place from which they come. Calvin, who is usually good at noting questions which other commentators ignore, simply says, 'As to the translation of the first words, it is literally many who sleep in the earth of dust, or who are in earth and dust . . .'[15]

3. The sentence could be taken to mean something like this: 'The many, namely those who sleep in the dust of the earth, will arise . . .'[16]

---

[14] J.G. Baldwin, *Daniel: An Introduction and Commentary* (TOTC; Leicester: IVP, 1978), 204; cf. also J. Jeremias, 'polloi', *Theological Dictionary of the New Testament* (ET; ed. G. Kittel and G. Friedrich, ET; Grand Rapids: Eerdmans, 1983), vol. 6, 536–45.

[15] J. Calvin, *Commentaries on the Book of the Prophet Daniel* (ET; Edinburgh: Calvin Translation Society, 1853), vol. 2, 373.

[16] Most commentators argue that the resurrection concerns 'many but not all', e.g. Goldingay, *Daniel*, 308; D.S. Russell, *Daniel. An Active Volcano* (Edinburgh: St. Andrews Press, 1989), 132; N. Porteous, *Daniel* (OTL; London: SCM, 1979), 170f. Those arguing for the meaning 'all' include H.C. Leupold, *Exposition of Daniel* (Welwyn: Evangelical Press, 1969[2], 529f.; R.S. Wallace, *The Lord is King: The Message of Daniel* (BST; Leicester: IVP, 1979), 194. E.J. Young, argues that 'all' represents a forced interpretation, but that the passage implies a general resurrection, *The Prophecy of Daniel: A Commentary* (Grand Rapids: Eerdmans, 1949), 256. W. Eichrodt says that 'This extension of the prophetic picture of judgment . . . means that the distinction between Israel and the heathen becomes almost meaningless as compared with their common liability to the divine retribution which is threatening all mankind, and thus comes close to the universalism of the early expectation of doom' (*Old Testament Theology* (London: SCM, 1964), vol. 1, 470f.).

The *minimum conclusion* is that this text proves that there is a belief in the Old Testament, though perhaps only at a late stage, that many or all of those who die are raised to life. The wicked are punished and the righteous are blessed. The text *might* be thought to allow a further group who are not raised to life.

Isaiah (25:8 and) 26:19

General Context

Isaiah 24 – 27 is usually reckoned to be a self-contained unit. Critical scholars often refer to it as the Isaiah Apocalypse – and also date it very late, e.g. the second century BC. This last conclusion need not be accepted, but we agree that the division is a logical one. Isaiah 13 – 23 deals with the nations around Judah from the eighth century onwards.[17] There are already several hints of a worldwide vision in these chapters (e.g. 13:6–13; 17:12–14; 19:24f.), but in chs. 24 – 7 the primary focus is the whole world, and the occasional mention of particular nations (Moab in 25:10–12; Leviathan = Egypt in 27:1, 12f.; Euphrates/Assyria in 27:12f.) serves to illustrate the effects of world judgment and salvation. The progression of thought in these chapters is as follows:

Chapter 24 is mostly a prophecy of world judgment with its climax in vv. 21 – 3: the Lord will punish the host of heaven, reign on Mount Zion, and manifest his glory before his elders. In the middle of this is a description of joy 'from the west' and a call to worship 'in the east' before the writer reverts to his own situation of distress (vv. 14–16).

Chapter 25 begins with a song of praise to God who has subdued ruthless nations. The prophet then moves into a remarkable (prose) prophecy which speaks of the destruction of death itself, and all peoples benefit from this action. *On that day* (v. 9) 'they' will acknowledge the action of God and issue a call to rejoice in him. The chapter ends with a picture of the humiliation of Moab. Two questions immediately arise:

---

[17] Babylon (chs. 13 – 14; and 21:1–10), Philistia (14:28–32), Moab (15 – 16), Syria (17), (beyond) Ethiopia (18), Egypt (19, with Assyria in verses 23–25), Babylon, Dumah, Arabia (21), Valley of vision and an individual, Shebna (22), Tyre (23).

1. What are the implications of this removal of death? Is it that a time is envisaged on earth in the future when people will no longer die, but those who have already died will be lost? Or is something more radical envisaged, viz. the restoration to life of those who are already dead? The prophet does not specify this, but he may be said to prepare for it. In other words this makes it more likely that 26:19 will yield evidence for belief in the resurrection of individuals. We should note that many scholars regard v. 8a as a gloss,[18] in which case it is regarded as outside the main train of thought of the section. However, it does fit well into its context. In other words, if it is a gloss it's a good one, and it is part of our canonical text.

2. Why Moab? Could it be that Moab is simply an example of a nation that has been opposed to God's purposes; has been haughty and now is humbled (16:6; cf. Edom in Isa. 34:1–17; 63:1–6; for Isaiah's strong emphasis on the danger of pride see ch. 2 especially)? This would be my view and that of many commentators. Motyer remarks, 'Moab is mentioned by name to remind us that eschatological disaster happens to real people.'[19]

Chapter 26 begins with a common introductory formula, 'in that day', linking it to what has gone before. The same formula

---

[18] The main reason for this is that the abolition of death is expressed 'in a monostich between the account of the abolition of the veil which revealed, and the removal of the tears from the face revealed', G.B. Gray, *Isaiah, I – XXVII* (ICC; Edinburgh: T. & T. Clark, 1928), 430 (referring also to Duhm); see also R.E. Clements, *Isaiah 1 – 39* (NCBC; Grand Rapids: Eerdmans, 1980), 208. The text does not in fact make such a close connection between removing the veil and removing tears.

[19] J.A. Motyer, *The Prophecy of Isaiah* (Leicester: IVP, 1993), 211. Clements (*Isaiah 1 – 39*, 210) and O. Kaiser (*Isaiah 13 – 39. A Commentary* (OTL; London: SCM, 1974), 202f.) regard this as a short addition to the text to exclude Moab from eventual salvation, due to some particularly anti-Moabite feeling at the time. This does not give an integrated explanation of the text as we have it. John Watts has a novel suggestion: 'Jerusalem is expected to behave so piously in the day of Yahweh's throne appearance. But instead the witnesses hear it claiming a petty right of sovereignty over its small neighbour, Moab. With childish glee it is demanding, in barnyard terms, the humiliation of Judah's former vassal.' See J.D.W. Watts, *Isaiah* (2 vols; WBC; Waco, Word 1985, 1987), vol. 1, 335.

continues the exposition in 27:1, 2 and 12.[20] Throughout the chapter there is a concern for trust in God, waiting upon the Lord only (vv. 8, 9, 13), and for 'righteousness.'

The text itself: 'thy dead shall live' (26.19)

Although this verse is somewhat difficult, it is not impossible to understand.[21] Literally, the prophet is speaking to Yahweh, as follows:

> Thy dead ones shall live (i.e. the dead ones of the people that belong to you, cf. Ps. 116:15)
>
> My body/carcase/corpse (singular, and assumed to be collective, i.e. the prophet's own people) shall arise (plural)
>
> Awake and shout for joy O dwellers in the dust
>
> For thy dew is a dew of light
>
> And land of shades will cause it to fall.

My body, corpse is apparently the right reading. RSV (etc.) emends on the basis of the Syriac and Targum, but it is an obvious word for alteration. A change in the vowel points alone would give 'my bodies.' Various explanations are offered for the reading 'body' but it seems necessary to accept that it is the correct reading and interpret it in a collective sense, parallel to 'dead ones' in the sentence preceding it.[22]

---

[20] The whole of Isa. 26 seems to be one 'song'. There are no strong division markers, but there are several features that imply a continuation of the same unit:
  verse 2, 'gates' depends on 'city' in v. 1.
  verse 5 again mentions 'the city'
  verses 3–4 introduce the themes of 'trust' and 'peace' which are continued in v. 12.

[21] See especially J.N. Oswalt, *The Book of Isaiah, chapters 1 – 39* (NICOT; Grand Rapids: Eerdmans, 1986), 486. Kaiser also has a useful discussion, although he regards this verse (and 25:8) as a late interpolation, *Isaiah 13 – 39*, 215–20.

[22] Clements suggests that *my body* suggests the influence of Ps. 49:15, and 'points to a later reading of the verse in reference to the resurrection of individuals', *Isaiah 1 – 39*, 216f.

The word *shades* (or 'ghosts') refers to the inhabitants of Sheol.[23] And we note that in v. 14 the two words 'dead' and 'shades' occur in parallel, and are said not to rise. Verse 19 forms a definite parallel and contrast with this. The other lords who did rule over us will not arise, but the ones in v. 19 will. Individuals would seem to be indicated in v. 14.

Scholarly views differ quite widely concerning the meaning of Isaiah 26:19. Gaster argues that 'the language is purely hyperbolic: the desired regeneration of a spiritually inert and virtually "dead" community of Israel is likened metaphorically and poetically to the quickening of languishing soil under the influence of even a slight morning drizzle.'[24] Martin-Achard is at pains to say how difficult the passage is, that it occurs in the latest strata of the Old Testament, and may be a gloss anyway. He concludes, however, that it does promise resurrection to those people who 'in an age of troubles and persecutions had been faithful, even to the point of giving their lives.'[25] Perhaps the majority of scholars are content to regard the passage as a prophecy of the rebirth of the Jewish community.[26]

Certainly one might argue that 'my body' refers to the nation, since it is a singular followed by a plural, and therefore must be taken collectively. Moreover, 'my' signifies that Yahweh is the speaker and there is no way to speak of *his* resurrection. If we accept this, we are still left with 'your dead (plural) shall live' and (Yahweh speaking) 'O dwellers in the dust (i.e. dead ones), awake and sing for joy.' This most naturally means that individuals are expected to come to life. The main reason for rejecting this explanation and going for a collective interpretation is the prior assumption that resurrection is not found in the Old Testament. I would grant that the text is not absolutely certain, but believe that by far the most likely interpretation is that it *does* prophesy the resurrection of individuals after death. The whole context of Isaiah 24–27 (including 25:8) strengthens the impression made by 26:19 alone.

---

[23] See also Job 26:5; Ps. 88:11; Prov. 2:18; 9:18; 21:16; Isa. 14:9; 26:14, 19.

[24] Gaster, 'Resurrection' in *IDB*, IV, 40.

[25] R. Martin-Achard, 'Resurrection (OT)' in *Anchor Bible Dictionary*, vol. 5, 680–4, on 682.

[26] See Clements, *Isaiah 1 – 39*, 216 (referring also to G. Fohrer and H. Wildberger).

Psalm 49

The strongest claim to evidence of life after death in the Psalter is to be found in Psalm 49. It seems to say that 'those with foolish confidence' will die and stay in the grave forever, but that God will ransom the Psalmist from the power of Sheol. Does it mean that he will literally be brought through the experience of death to live in God's presence? Or is it simply that he expects God to stop him falling into the power of Sheol (i.e. dying)? I believe that the former view may be shown to be right. The general outline of the Psalm is as follows:[27]

> Verses 1–4: Introduction: an invitation to all peoples to listen to the teaching. These verses tell us that what follows is puzzling and demands vigorous thought.
>
> Verses 5–12: The personal question: 'Why should *I* fear . . . rich and powerful enemies?' The answer is given *indirectly* by mentioning some pertinent information: all of them will eventually die; their money can't provide a ransom for their lives. This is more like a treatise than a testimony.
>
> Verses 13–15: The climax and turning point: reiterates and confirms the fate of those who are confident in this life (cf. v. 6), but a twist is introduced (without which the Psalm does not contain much comfort): the wicked die and are lost for ever, but God will ransom me from death.
>
> Verses 16–20 return to the same subject matter as vv. 5–12 but, instead of the first person question, 'Why should I fear?', we have a second-person imperative, 'Do not fear.' There is again a discussion of human beings as mortal: even the rich die, and the Psalm concludes with a confident exhortation not to fear the rich. (Implicitly these verses draw attention to the fact that God remains in control of the whole situation.)

---

[27] Following the division markers: the refrain which ends both vv. 5–12 and vv. 16–20; the *Selah* which marks out vv. 13 and 15. Textual difficulties, especially in vv. 7, 13 and 14, present problems for all interpreters (see the detailed commentaries for discussion). My own suggestion for v. 14 would be:
> (Like) sheep they are appointed for Sheol; death will shepherd them, and the righteous (will have) ruled over them in the morning (= resurrection morning? cf. Ps. 17:15). Sheol, rather than a lofty abode, will be theirs.

For a helpful treatment see P.S. Johnston, 'Psalm 49: A Personal Eschatology' in *'The reader must understand': Eschatology in Bible and Theology* (eds. K.E. Brower and M.W. Elliott; Leicester: Apollos (IVP), 1997), 73–84.

Verse 15, 'God will ransom my soul from the power of Sheol, for he will receive me', is obviously the key verse in this discussion. There are two main ways of viewing its meaning within the overall argument of the Psalm. Some regard it as a counterpart to vv. 5–6: the Lord rescues the Psalmist from premature death (the 'sphere of Sheol'), not from Sheol itself after he has died. Verse 10a, of course, makes the point that everyone dies, the wise as well as the stupid.[28] Others note, however, the consequence of God's ransoming the psalmist from death is that 'God will receive me.' This uses the same verb as is used Genesis 5:24 (of Enoch) and 2 Kings 2:5 (of Elijah). In Psalm 73:24 the same verb 'take (away)' or 'receive' is found in a similar context, strengthening the view that *both* psalms refer to life after death. On this view v. 15 is to be thought of as the counterpart to v. 7. In some Hebrew manuscripts both are introduced by the same Hebrew word. This means that, while the rich cannot ransom themselves, the Lord will ransom the Psalmist.

We would not expect the Psalmist to have a very clear idea of life after death, but he has the sort of conviction seen in Job 19:25–7, that he will not perish after death. Weiser states: 'How this will come to pass the author does not explain. This is something hidden from the eyes of mortal man; but it suffices to have the assurance that God will take care of man after his death and does not abandon him to the power of the underworld.'[29]

Our interpretation of this psalm must be based upon the overall thrust and shape of the psalm, and is not overthrown by detailed study of the textual difficulties. In other words, despite the uncertainty of some words and phrases, it is highly probable that the psalmist makes a distinction between the wicked who go to and remain in Sheol, and the righteous (including himself) whom God will ransom from Sheol. H.W. Wolff's conclusion is worth quoting: 'The overcoming of death's agony is not manifested in any elaborate hope of the beyond, but in the calm

---

[28] H.-J. Kraus, *Psalms 1 – 59* (Minneapolis: Augsburg, 1988), 484f. (quoting C. Barth).
[29] See A. Weiser, *The Psalms* (OTL; London: SCM, 1962), 389f. (well worth reading throughout).

certainty that the communion with Yahweh cannot be ended by death, because of his faithfulness.'[30]

Job 19:25–7

Job 19:25–6 is precious to many millions of Christians. It is used at funeral services; it has been set to music – in Handel's *Messiah* and in the hymn 'I know that my Redeemer lives'; it has inspired many to hope again when they had lost all hope. It has therefore come as a terrible shock to many to read some of the new translations of these verses. So the REB has:

> I know that my vindicator lives
>
> and that he will rise last to speak in court . . .

Not only is the rhythm gone; so is the hope of resurrection. Many modern scholars would agree with this type of interpretation. For example, Gaster writes: 'The famous words . . . "I know" [rather "If only I knew"] that my Redeemer lives . . . express a desperate hope for the impossible a – *cri de coeur* – rather than a confidence in the inevitable.'[31]

In the face of so much disagreement we must try to determine the range of possible translations and interpret the passage in the light of its context, taking account of the significance of the terms used. It is not quoted in the New Testament, so we have no information from that quarter.

Verses 23–4 lead into the verses in question. Job expresses the hope that his words might be made into a permanent record, inscribed into the rock and filled with lead (so as not to be worn away and made illegible). They make it clear that Job's main concern is for vindication. We shall treat verse 25 phrase by phrase:

For I know that my go'el lives/is alive

The word *go'el* is used of the kinsman redeemer who buys back the property of an impoverished relative. So Boaz acted as *go'el*

---

[30] *Anthropology of the Old Testament* (London: SCM, 1974), 109.
[31] Gaster, 'Resurrection' in *Interpreter's Dictionary of the Bible*, vol. 4, 40.

in redeeming Naomi's property – and marrying Ruth at the same time (in order to 'raise up sons for the dead man'). The word means, therefore, 'someone who rescues from a plight about which a person can do nothing.' We note also the legal implications of the term: Boaz settled the matter before the elders at the city gate, the local court of justice. The sort of case that NEB/REB envisages goes beyond this type of agreement, but it was the duty of the *go'el* to plead the cause of his wronged relative in court, as in Jeremiah 50:34; Proverbs 23:10–11; cf. Psalm 119:154; Lamentations 3:58–59.

The word is also used to denote the person whose duty it was to 'avenge the blood' of a relative who had been wrongly killed (Num. 35:19). Since the only one whom Job accuses of causing his plight is God, it seems unlikely that this meaning is primary here. No one is going to put God to death for manslaughter. Verses 28–9, however, speak of punishment for those who pursue Job.

Job wants two things: first, to be shown to have been in the right – hence the reference in vv. 23–4 to the indelible inscription of Job's words; and second, to be delivered from his predicament – and restored to fellowship with God once more? This desire is suggested in v. 26 'I shall see God.' So we could argue that the *go'el* is a suitable concept for both these ideas.[32]

---

[32] Who is this *go'el*? The term *go'el* is used of the Lord, particularly as redeemer of the people from slavery in Egypt (e.g. Exod. 6:6; 15:13; Pss. 74:2; 77:15); and Isaiah 40 – 55 uses it to describe the deliverance of Judah from Babylon (e.g. 43:1–7; cf. 41:14; 44:24; 49:7–9, 26). Most commentators therefore assume it to be God, but some find difficulty in the concept of God witnessing for him when the judge must be God. So they assume it to be the heavenly witness mentioned in 16:19 (cf. 9:33–4 where, however, he seems to hold out no hope of finding such an umpire). This 'witness' seems clearly to be different from God since his task is to be a witness for Job towards God (cf. especially v. 11). The figure appears mysteriously and is difficult to interpret, but perhaps the best analogy is to think of some sort of opposing counterpart to Satan (cf. Zech. 3:1–5 where the 'angel of the Lord' stands by and takes part in Joshua's justification). The word that occurs parallel to 'witness' ('one ready to answer for me', NIV; 'he that vouches for', RSV) seems to be an Aramaic loanword, the root of which occurs elsewhere only in Gen. 31:47, where the Hebrew and Aramaic names of the heap of witness between Jacob and Laban are given.

and that he shall stand up at the last upon the dust (=earth)

'Dust' probably signifies that the action has to take place down here on earth, where all the action has been, and where Job's name is slandered. 'Last' has occasioned many different views. The closest analogy with our present passage is in Isaiah 48:12, 'I am the first and I am *the last*', and 44:6, 'Thus says the Lord, the King of Israel and his *go'el*, the Lord of hosts: I am the first and I am *the last*.' This would mean translating: 'and *as the last (one)* he shall rise upon the earth.'[33]

Is this the only possibility? Well several ancient versions and some modern commentators have understood it to mean 'at the last time' or 'at last' (i.e. when the final end comes, or simply 'eventually'). In addition, some scholars have noted that the parallel with Isaiah 40 – 55 is not exact: there is no definite article here. Moreover, the word can be construed as either an adjective ('a last one') or an accusative of state.[34]

Verse 26 is also very difficult to translate with assurance. Literally it says:

> And after [or afterwards] – my skin – they have struck off/ surrounded – this!

> And from [looking out from (= 1. or 3. below) or outside of (= 2. below)?]

> my flesh I shall see God.

The ancient versions translate it very differently, which shows, as Dhorme remarks, 'that the difficulties did not arise yesterday'![35] The main interpretations are these:

> 1. After death Job will, as a spirit, see his vindication by God. This is not a Hebraic way of thinking and it seems unlikely (see also 14:21).

> 2. God will intervene before Job's death to vindicate him; i.e. he will be emaciated (skin off) but still alive. This interpretation does

[33] Noting that 'rise' is used of rising to speak as a witness (cf. 16:8; Ps. 76:9), we can see where the REB gets its translation from.
[34] A.E. Cowley, *Gesenius' Hebrew Grammar as edited and enlarged by the late E. Kautzsch* (Oxford: Clarendon, 1910[2]), see 'last', 118 n.
[35] E. Dhorme, *A Commentary on the Book of Job* (ET; Nashville: Nelson, 1967[2]), 284.

not fit well with vv. 23f. where Job asks that his words might be inscribed with an iron pen, presumably as a witness when he is no longer able to speak in person.

3. God will raise Job from the grave and vindicate him; i.e. Job will see God after death (after his skin has gone completely). The main difficulty is to reconcile this with Job's statements elsewhere (7:9; 10:21; 14:10–12; 17:15–16). However, the book itself indicates a fluctuation in Job's feelings and confidence (cf. also 6:26, 'the speech of a despairing man is wind').

What can we be sure of, apart from the fact that this is difficult to translate? Well, we cannot be absolutely sure that Job refers to the resurrection. Perhaps Job himself would not have known exactly how he would be able to witness his vindication. But he does have the conviction that it will come. As Hartley remarks, the reasoning that lies behind Job's conviction is the same that leads to the Christian hope of resurrection: God is just, and however things appear, the person who is righteous before him will never be abandoned.[36] It is impossible that Job can die and simply cease to exist. Rowley's comment seems to be justified: 'Job's leap of faith reaches, but does not securely grasp, this thought [i.e. of resurrection].'[37]

4. The Resurrection of the Messiah

Isaiah 52:13 – 53:12

There are many problems in interpreting the details of this famous 'chapter' but its overall thrust is clear and powerful. It describes the servant of the Lord, from his humiliation and death – a death for others – to his final exaltation. Both Jews and Christians at first regarded this passage as a prophecy of the Messiah, but Jews rejected this option because of the way that Christians used it for apologetic and polemical purposes.[38]

[36] J.E. Hartley, *Job* (NICOT; Grand Rapids: Eerdmans, 1988), 295–7.
[37] H.H. Rowley, *Job* (NCBC; London: Marshall, Morgan & Scott, 1980), 137.
[38] See J. Jeremias, 'Pais Theou' in *TDNT*, V, 686–700; S.H.T. Page, 'The Suffering Servant Between the Testaments', *New Testament Studies* 31 (1985), 481–97.

Instead they adopted (usually) a corporate interpretation – the servant is Israel – or else referred it to some other individual. Recent commentators have espoused a number of different interpretations. Perhaps the clearest and one of the best known is that of R.N. Whybray who regards this section as a 'thanksgiving of a liberated prophet.'[39] The prophet was in prison in Babylon and nearly died; however, he recovered and wrote this prayer of thanksgiving. The ingenuity required to establish this view is remarkable.

Martin-Achard also denies that the text speaks of the resurrection of an individual: 'The passage poses difficult problems and there is no clear evidence that this text can be numbered among those which testify in favour of resurrection.' He deals with the possibilities of a community interpretation, in which case there is no question of individual death or resurrection, and with individual interpretation,[40] in which case 'the essence of this chapter consists not in the special lot that awaits the servant after his suffering, but in the fact that God's plan is realized through him and that this is recognized as such.' This is surely a fudging of what the text actually says: the servant was cut off from the land of the living, he poured out his soul to death and made his grave with the wicked etc. – but he is given a portion with the great and divides the spoil with the strong – after this event.

---

[39] R.N. Whybray, *Thanksgiving for a Liberated Prophet: An Interpretation of Isaiah Chapter 53* (Sheffield: Sheffield Academic Press, 1978); see also *Isaiah 40 – 66* (NCBC; London: Marshall, Morgan & Scott, 1975), 169–83. All the difficulties of an individual interpretation 'are removed . . . when it is realized that the supposed references to the Servant's vicarious suffering and death are illusory, due partly to a misunderstanding of the language of a particular kind of religious poetry and partly to the determination of Christian interpreters to find here a prefiguration of the suffering, death and resurrection of Christ' (171f.). Be that as it may, Jewish commentators generally went for the individual interpretation until well into the Christian era.

[40] 'Resurrection (OT)' in *Anchor Bible Dictionary*, vol. 5, 682. He states: 'If, however, the referent is an individual, some member of the community who suffers for others and notably for his brothers, the expressions employed in Is. 53 do not automatically imply that the servant is to be put to death, and his final victory (evoked in vv. 10–12) does not demand that he be snatched from death. The essence of the message in this chapter consists not in the special lot that awaits the servant after his suffering . . .' This view is difficult to square with the emphatic clarity of the text on the death of the Servant and his ultimate exaltation.

We shall focus our discussion on those parts of the passage that are of most relevance for the present study. Verses 13–15 are usually regarded as a preface to ch. 53; the basis for this is readily apparent: 'my servant' is the person referred to in both; the exalted status of the servant is noted at the end of each; the similarity in the thoughts expressed in 52:15b and 53:1a. They are, I believe, a strong indication of the unity of 52:13–53:12, and most commentators agree.[41] Verse 15 contains a word that is difficult to translate: will the servant startle or sprinkle many nations? Whatever we choose, the thought is of a transformation from a low to an exalted state, and a corresponding change of mind in the nations and kings.[42] It is clear that this is in harmony with the movement of thought in ch. 53.

The beginning of ch. 53 is comparatively clear. There is some doubt about the meaning of two Hebrew terms (which occur in vv. 3 and 4), which leads to some uncertainty whether the servant was a man of 'sorrows' or 'pains', and acquainted with 'grief' or 'sickness.' In view of the clarification in vv. 5–8, we need not worry too much about the choice. The servant bears the iniquity of 'us all.'

Verse 8 describes him as 'cut off from the land of the living.' Whybray comments: 'Taken literally, this phrase almost certainly means that the servant died. But a literal translation is not mandatory.' He quotes Lamentations 3:54, 'I am cut off', where the same verb (g-z-r) occurs and where the speaker is obviously not dead. There, however, the text contains a clear indication of the figurative nature of the speech, and there is no emphasis on 'the land of the living.' Verse 9 has some odd features. It is literally:

'And they appointed [gave] his grave with the wicked

and with a rich man in his *deaths*

although or *because* he had done no violence . . .'

---

[41] Whybray denies it on the basis that 52:13–15 is spoken by Yahweh and can hardly be a preface to the prophet's song of thanksgiving in ch. 53. This is hardly compelling. See C. Westermann, *Isaiah 40 – 66* (OTL; London: SCM, 1969), 255–8, for a helpful discussion.

[42] The problem is to identify the root from which the word (*yazzeh*) comes. The LXX has 'many nations shall be astonished at him'.

The verse is not difficult to translate; the difficulty is to understand why the different expressions are put together and to define the logical connection between them. 'Deaths' may be taken as a plural of majesty: 'his supreme death.' There is no need to emend the text to read 'his burial mound.'[43]

Verse 10 is difficult, astounding even, but the words make sense:

> And/but the Lord was pleased to crush him,
>
> he has put him to grief [the same root that we saw in vv. 3 and 4 that yields the word meaning 'grief' or 'sickness'].
>
> When you make his soul [to be] a sin offering[44]
>
> he will see his seed, he will prolong his days
>
> the pleasure [the same root as in 10a] of the Lord will prosper in his hands.

Verse 11 is fairly straightforward, but we note the occurrence of the word 'justify': 'a just one, my servant, will justify.'[45] The phrase 'bear their iniquities' *could* mean 'suffer because of their sin' (without any vicarious atonement) as in Lamentations 5:7, but this is hardly possible when it comes straight after 'will justify many', and when the context of the whole chapter speaks of the Lord's action in laying 'our sins' on the servant.

The thought of these verses is amazing. Nowhere else in Scripture is there countenanced the possibility of a human being giving his life as a sin-offering for others. Child sacrifice was regarded as an abomination, or 'causing one's children to pass through the fire.' Yet the idea is there in the sacrificial system: an animal dies instead of, or in the place of, sinful people. The idea of bearing iniquity vicariously seems to be expressed in Numbers 18:1–2, where Aaron and his sons bear iniquity in connection

---

[43] See especially Motyer, *Isaiah*, 435f.
[44] See F. Brown, S.R. Driver, and C.A. Briggs, *A Hebrew and English Lexicon of the Old Testament* (Oxford: OUP, 1907), 79f. The word can mean 'offence, guilt, compensation' but most frequently, as here, it means sin-offering or trespass-offering. It occurs in Leviticus, Numbers and Ezekiel, and in 1 Sam. 6 and 2 Kgs. 12:17.
[45] *Hiphil* of *ts-d-q*. See M. Butterworth, 'Justification in the Old Testament' in J.I. Packer and Others, *Here We Stand* (London: Hodder & Stoughton, 1986).

with the sanctuary. There is no good reason for a confessing Christian to have any doubts about the witness of this text to the resurrection of the Messiah. We might still quibble about whether others share in this. The answer to this comes easily from other passages of the Bible.

Psalm 16:9–11

The general consensus among commentators has been that the psalmist here expresses the hope that he will escape from the danger that he faces at the current time and will not die. It does not, therefore, express anything like a resurrection hope. This does seem to be the main thrust of the psalm, but there have been powerful advocates of a deeper understanding than this. Philip Johnston argues that Sheol is thought of as the destination of the wicked, and the psalmist believes that he will escape this. He has no clear idea of what the alternative must be, except that he believes he will continue in communion with Yahweh.[46] Weiser argues that the psalmist is 'progressing towards the conquest of the fear of death.' He says it is *possible* that he may be thinking of resurrection from the dead, since the word rendered 'pit' is derived from the root 'to decay', which would accord well with the LXX and Acts 2:25ff.; 13:35. It is more likely, however, that he wants to avoid identifying with pagan beliefs in resurrection, but affirms that life lived in communion with God leads to victory over death.[47] This view is strengthened by v. 11. These views seem attractive, but perhaps not overwhelmingly persuasive.[48] Nevertheless it is right to draw attention to the focus of the Psalmist's attention: *The Lord* is his only good, his chosen portion and cup, the one who is always before him and because of whom he will not be moved (Ps. 16:2, 5, 8). Surely there is at least a glimpse beyond this life.

Psalm 17:15

This is the last verse of a psalm which *may* be the prayer of an accused man (vv. 1–5, +? 8ff.) who has taken refuge in the

---

[46] 'Left in Hell?', 213–22.
[47] Weiser, *Psalms*, 177f.
[48] See also W. Eichrodt, *Theology of the Old Testament*, vol. 2, 524; von Rad, *Old Testament Theology* , vol. 1, 402ff.

temple (vv. 6–7). There are two main types of interpretation (yet again) here. They are:

1. 'Awake' indicates awaking from death. The same Hebrew verb (*q-y-ts*) is used in Isaiah 26:19 and Daniel 12:2. However, the verb is also used of awaking from natural sleep (Isa. 29:8; Jer. 31:26). Even the fact that the same root is used in Ezek. 7:6 in connection with judgment: 'An end [*qets* from the root *q-ts-ts*] has come, the end has come, it has awakened against you', does not give firm support to this as the primary interpretation. The same verb is used in Psalm 139:18, 'when I awake I am still with you', in a comparable context, but the context contains no indication that an eschatological meaning is intended.[49]

2. Verses 3 and 15 signify that the psalmist has 'spent the night in the sanctuary and that in the morning he was given the divine answer which may have been communicated to him by means of an oracle.'[50] This is not irresistible either, but it is reasonable.

5. Conclusions

Ancient Israelites were strongly discouraged from speculation concerning the dead, and encouraged to give maximum attention to this world. Those who had lived a good life and reached a good age could be satisfied with that. The important things were to live in faithfulness to God, remembering his great acts of love and mercy on behalf of his people. In areas where they were ignorant, they were not to speculate but to trust. The Israelite of old was not granted a clear vision of life beyond the grave.

This suggests that it is not such a bad thing when people find it difficult to believe in life after death. I find this comforting because I do find it difficult to believe with my imagination and

---

[49] RSV offers a marginal reading 'were I to come to an end', but this is based on an emendation of the pointing, which implies a different verb: *q-ts-ts* again.
[50] A.A. Anderson, *Psalms* (NCBC; London: Marshall, Morgan & Scott, 1972), vol. 1, 147.

my heart that one day I shall be alive in God's presence. I have no difficulty in assenting to it, or in believing intellectually. It's just difficult to take in. And for some it's more difficult.

Nevertheless, there are preparations for a doctrine of resurrection in the Old Testament. It is not that later thinkers had to contradict what earlier ones had said. No, there are indications in the earliest strata of the Old Testament that life with God can exist in places other than on earth. The Old Testament presents a world in which life after death is not only possible, but necessary. Sooner or later those who live by Old Testament traditions will have to realize that life with God continues beyond the grave. From time to time there are glimpses of this conviction.

The teaching found in the Old Testament encourages the development of a doctrine of resurrection rather than of the immortality of the soul. It encourages a holistic and down-to-earth attitude towards human living. It focuses our minds on what is here and now as of great significance within God's overall purposes.

Finally, when we have doubts today about things we cannot see, the solution is not to spend vast amounts of time looking at arguments for resurrection. The solution is God. To draw close to the source of all life. 'To know him and the power of his resurrection', as Paul put it in Philippians 3:10.

Questions for further study

1. Why is the Old Testament more concerned with the events of this life than our future existence?

2. How might the interpretation of Daniel 12.1f influence our interpretation of the other passages discussed in this chapter?

3. How persuasive is the minimum conclusion that the Old Testament *does* affirm personal continuity of existence after death?

4. What connections could be made between the teaching of the Old Testament and that of the New Testament on the subject of the general resurrection?

5. In what ways is the resurrection of the Messiah as depicted in Isaiah (and the Psalms?) picked up in the New Testament?

Select Bibliography

Alexander, T.D., 'The Psalms and the Afterlife', *Irish Biblical Studies* 9 (1987), 2–17

Barr, J., *The Garden of Eden and the Hope of Immortality: The Read-Tueckwell Lecture for 1990* (London: SCM, 1992)

Eichrodt, W., *Theology of the Old Testament* (London: SCM, 1967), especially vol. 2, 496–529

Johnston, Philip S., 'Left in Hell? Psalm 16, Sheol and the Holy One' in P.S. Satterthwaite, R.S. Hess, and G.J. Wenham, *The Lord's Anointed* (Carlisle: Paternoster, 1995), 213–22

Kaiser, O. and Lohse, E., *Death and Life* (ET; J.E. Steely; Nashville: Abingdon, 1981)

Martin-Achard, R., 'Resurrection (OT)' in *Anchor Bible Dictionary* (New York: Doubleday, 1992), 680–4

Two

Resurrection Apologetics and the Theology of Luke–Acts

DAVID PETERSON

1. Introduction

Conservative apologists for the resurrection of Jesus often use the biblical material to establish two main points: the divinity of Christ and the certainty that believers will share eternal life with him. Although such arguments can be developed from Luke–Acts, this study shows how the author sets Jesus' resurrection within the broader context of scriptural teaching about God's saving plan for Israel and the nations. In different ways, the resurrection is used to challenge the beliefs and hopes of a variety of first-century audiences. It is clearly a key to Luke's christology and soteriology, but in a more profound sense than is recognized by much contemporary preaching on the subject.

Liberal scholars have other reasons for narrowing the scope and application of biblical teaching about the resurrection of Jesus. For example, with an eye to the scepticism of modern readers, Leslie Houlden has recently made a plea for the validity of a 'resurrectionless Christianity.' He concedes that in the book of Acts the resurrection is 'the clear differentiating point of Christianity' and 'the key to salvation',[1] but insists that Luke

---

[1] L. Houlden, 'The Resurrection and Christianity', *Theology* 99: 789 (May/June 1996), 198–205 (203).

does not dwell on the resurrection itself but 'turns quickly aside to show how Jesus is to be validated (or validate himself) from Scripture and how he is to be known in breaking bread.' He also notes that in Acts the resurrection becomes, in effect, 'an incident on the way to the ascended glory.'[2] There is some truth in these observations, but Houlden uses them to play down the significance of the resurrection itself. It is not adequate to say that Luke somehow moves beyond 'the basic if enigmatic story he took from Mark', just because his narrative becomes absorbed with some of the deeper implications of Jesus' resurrection.

The offence of a doctrine of physical resurrection in the Greco-Roman world demanded the sort of comprehensive apologetic that Luke gives us at the end of his Gospel and in the Acts of the Apostles. Instead of avoiding this issue for Gentile readers, Luke confronted it by the way he presented his evidence. We shall also note how much his apologetic is geared for *Jewish* audiences, challenging them to believe that Jesus of Nazareth is the Messiah.

2. The foundational importance of Luke 24

Most of this paper will be devoted to an examination of the book of Acts, but some brief observations must first be made about the way the evidence for Jesus' resurrection is selected and presented in the last chapter of Luke's Gospel. In both volumes of his work, Luke is concerned to demonstrate the reality and significance of Jesus' bodily resurrection. Acts begins with a summary statement to the effect that Jesus presented himself alive after his suffering 'by many convincing proofs' (1:3).[3] Luke 24 records the evidence of the empty tomb and the angelic

---

[2] Ibid. 204. For different perspectives on the relationship between the resurrection and ascension of Jesus, cf. R.F. O'Toole, 'Luke's understanding of Jesus' resurrection-ascension-exaltation', *Biblical Theology Bulletin* 9 (1979), 106–14.

[3] *Tekmērion* means 'strict proof' or 'a compelling sign' in Greek literature. The word only occurs here in the NT. Luke could not have chosen a stronger term to convey the sense of proof beyond doubt, cf. G.T.D. Angel '*tekmērion*', *The New International Dictionary of New Testament Theology* (3 vols,; ed. C. Brown; Exeter: Paternoster, 1978) (Henceforth: NIDNTT) vol. 3, 571.

witness to Jesus' resurrection before highlighting three such appearances. The evangelist links them so that they all seem to have happened on Easter Day, in and around Jerusalem. The redemption promised to Israel (Lk. 24:21; 1:68; 2:38; cf. 21:28) is thus shown to have been accomplished at its heart. From Jerusalem, salvation then goes out to the Gentiles, as predicted in Scripture (24:45–7).

The first resurrection appearance is to Cleopas and his companion on the road to Emmaus (vv. 13–33), the second to Simon (reported briefly in v. 34), and the third to the Eleven and 'their companions' (vv. 33–51). Acts 1 suggests that there were other such appearances and that they took place 'during forty days' (cf. 13:31; 1 Cor. 15:5–7).[4] One of the aims of these encounters, as Luke saw them, was to demonstrate the physical reality of Jesus' resurrection. So we are told that Jesus invited them to touch him and that he ate and drank in their presence (cf. Lk. 24:36–43; cf. Acts 10:41). He was no phantom and their experience was not simply visionary or spiritual.

Nevertheless, the Emmaus story suggests that even a resurrection appearance was not sufficient to convince those whose eyes were 'kept from recognizing him' (v. 16). God must open such eyes to perceive from the Scriptures the necessity for the Messiah to suffer and enter his glory by resurrection (vv. 25–32, 44–7). This is an important preparation for the resurrection apologetic that appears in the sermons in Acts.

The last scene in Luke 24 is also relevant for understanding the perspective of Acts. Unambiguously, v. 34 indicates that all the assembled disciples believed by this stage that Jesus had risen from the dead. What follows in vv. 36–43, however, is designed to establish the physical and empirical reality of the risen Jesus.[5] His words in vv. 44–7 then function to open their eyes to the saving significance of his death and resurrection,

---

[4] The evangelist presents the women as the first witnesses of the resurrection in the sense that they observe the empty tomb and hear the angelic testimony which affirms that Jesus' prediction has been fulfilled (Lk. 24:1–11). Cf. J. Plevnik, 'The Eyewitnesses of the Risen Jesus in Luke 24', *Catholic Biblical Quarterly* 49 (1987), 90–103 (esp. 91–3).

[5] S. Brown rightly observes that 'the object of *apistountōn* in v. 41 is not the resurrection itself but the *corporeal nature* of the resurrection' (*Apostasy and Perseverance in the Theology of St. Luke* (Analecta Biblica 36; Rome: Biblical Institute, 1969), 79).

through the Scriptures and with reference to his own predictions. The revelation to the disciples at the end of Luke 24 repeats what has previously been shown to those at the tomb and to those bound for Emmaus. This happens so that the Eleven can become *authentic witnesses* to the resurrection (v. 48).

> As the appointed witnesses, the eleven and those with them must see *for themselves* the risen Jesus. They must verify *on their own* that present among them is indeed the Jesus who had been with them before his death and who had died on the cross. As witnesses *they themselves must hear directly* from the lips of the risen Jesus the explanation of his own prediction and of the Scriptures. This they do only after they had verified and accepted his real presence among them. Moreover, the meaning of the death and resurrection of Christ is not to be their own derivation from the Scriptures but is to be given to them, i.e., revealed.[6]

Luke 24 concludes with the ascension of Jesus and the declaration that the disciples worshipped him (v. 52; cf. Matt. 28:9, 16).[7] This is the first time in Luke's Gospel that such terminology is used to describe the response of disciples of Jesus (cf. 4:7, 8). Although it is not the first real expression of faith in his resurrection, such a response at this climactic point in the narrative suggests some development in their thinking about him. 'Easter faith' for Luke perhaps involves two stages: belief in the reality of Jesus' resurrection and then, more fully, an acknowledgement of his divinity.[8]

The sermons in Acts are clearly designed to bring people to that fullness of faith in the resurrected and ascended Lord. Indeed, Jesus' resurrection, ascension and enthronement are closely linked in Luke's theology as they are in Hebrews. But this does not mean that belief in a physical resurrection is somehow of less significance in Luke–Acts or that it is subsumed by ascension and enthronement emphases.

---

[6] Plevnik, 'The Eyewitnesses', 101.

[7] The textual evidence for including *proskynēsantes* ('worshipped') in Lk. 24:52 is quite strong. Although the reading is missing from representatives of the Western text, this is not a sufficient reason for doubting that it was part of the original. Cf. B.M. Metzger (ed.), *A Textual Commentary on the Greek New Testament* (London/New York: United Bible Societies, 1971), 190–3.

[8] Cf. Plevnik, 'The Eyewitnesses', 103.

3. The apostles as witnesses of the resurrection

The two volumes of Luke's work are closely linked together by a focus on the preparation of the apostles to be witnesses of the risen and ascended Lord Jesus. We are first told in Acts 1 about his instructions through the Holy Spirit (v. 2) and his speaking to them about the kingdom of God (v. 3). More specifically, his instruction is the command to wait in Jerusalem for the gift of the Spirit (vv. 4–5). The themes of kingdom, Spirit and witness are developed and interconnected in vv. 6–8, where the ground plan for the book is laid out. The ascension makes possible Jesus' heavenly enthronement as Messiah, guaranteeing that he will remain sovereign over the life and witness of his people. The manner of his departure also foreshadows his return to consummate God's saving plan (vv. 9–11). In effect, the preface lays down 'the eschatological framework within which the Christian story is to unfold.'[9]

The last half of Acts 1 is devoted to the matter of making up the number of the Twelve. This was presumably important so that the disciples could represent in their number the ideal of a reunited and renewed people of God – Israel in its fullness, not just a remnant (cf. Lk. 22:28–30; Ezek. 37:15–28; Rev. 21:12, 14).[10] Here, for the first time in Acts, Old Testament citations are used to justify and explain the outworking of the divine plan, which included the betrayal of Jesus by one of his closest friends and the need to replace Judas with another.

Peter declares in 1:21–2 that being a witness of the resurrection was a vital qualification for apostleship. Consequently, the resurrection assumes a central place in the apostolic preaching (e.g. Acts 2:24–36; 4:33; 13:30–7). Yet such witnesses needed to be 'one of the men who have accompanied us during all the time that the Lord Jesus went in and out among us, beginning from the baptism of John until the day when he

---

[9] C.K. Barrett, *A Critical and Exegetical Commentary on the Acts of the Apostles* (2 vols; ICC; Edinburgh: T. & T. Clark, 1994), vol. 1, 63.

[10] Several commentators note the parallel in 1QS8.1, where 12 leaders appear to represent the Qumran community as the true or renewed Israel, final authority resting with a smaller body of two or three. Cf. R.N. Longenecker, *Biblical Exegesis in the Apostolic Period* (Grand Rapids: Eerdmans, 1981), 265.

was taken up from us.'[11] With such a perspective on the person
and work of Christ, the Twelve had a particular advantage and
could be guarantors of the whole gospel tradition (cf. Mt. 28:20).
In terms of Luke's prologue, this enabled them to be both
'eyewitnesses' and 'servants of the word' (Lk. 1:2), that is, those
qualified to interpret and explain the things to which they
testified.

4. Jesus as the resurrected saviour-king of David's line

The centrality of Jesus' resurrection to the apostolic preaching is
first exemplified in Acts 2. Peter begins by proclaiming the
coming of the Spirit as an eschatological event – the beginning
of the fulfilment of God's ancient promise in Joel 2:28–32 (cf.
Acts 2:14–21). The prior cause of the pentecostal event is then
shown to be the resurrection and ascension of the Messiah to the
right hand of God (2:22–35). Scripture is used to explain and
justify these assertions. God is shown to be the hidden actor
behind Jesus' mighty works (v. 22), his death (v. 23), his
resurrection (vv. 24, 32), his exaltation and the giving of the
Spirit (vv. 33–4), and his enthronement as Lord and Christ
(v. 36). Peter then challenges his hearers to change their
perception of Jesus, to share the convictions of his followers and
their experience of the Holy Spirit (2:36–40). Although charged
with rejecting the Messiah, the crowd is given another chance to
share in the salvation promised to Israel.

   In many ways, the sermon in Acts 2 is programmatic for the
events to follow and for understanding the apostolic preaching
in subsequent chapters. Peter's witness as a Spirit-empowered
apostle inaugurates the first stage in the fulfilment of Jesus'
mission plan (1:8). His preaching not only explains the anointing
with the Spirit of the initial core of disciples but also causes

---

[11] The period indicated here is that covered in the apostolic preaching (e.g.
Acts 10:37–42; 13:24–31). The expression in 1:22 cannot be pressed too
literally, since it appears from Luke's Gospel that not all of the apostles were
with Jesus from the very beginning. In simple terms, the candidates needed to
have been with Jesus throughout the span of his ministry. Cf. R.C. Tannehill,
*The Narrative Unity of Luke–Acts: A Literary Interpretation, Volume 2, The Acts
of the Apostles* (Minneapolis: Fortress, 1990), 23.

many Jews 'from every nation under heaven' to turn in repentance and faith to Jesus as Lord and Christ and receive the gift of the Spirit themselves.

The pouring out of God's Spirit

According to Joel 2:28–32, the pouring out of the Spirit 'upon all flesh' is a sign of the nearness of the End. Since 'the Lord's great and glorious day' is approaching, it is time for people to 'call on the name of the Lord' for salvation. In one sense, the rest of Peter's sermon is designed to show that *Jesus is the Lord on whom they are to call* (vv. 22–36; cf. Rom. 10:9–13) and to explain that calling upon his name means submitting in repentance and faith to baptism in his name (vv. 37–9; cf. 22:16).

The contrast between God's exaltation of Jesus and the attitude of those who opposed him is a central aspect of the apostolic preaching (cf. 2:36; 3:14–15; 4:10; 5:30; 10:39–40; 13:28–30). Jesus' resurrection was *his ultimate accreditation and vindication as God's servant and Messiah*. The latter point comes out emphatically as Peter begins to demonstrate the fulfilment of David's words (Acts 2:25–36). When it is claimed that God freed Jesus from 'the pains of death' (2:24, NRSV marg.), because it was impossible for him to be 'held in its power', a word that normally applies to the 'agony' of childbirth is used (*tas ōdinas*, 'the birthpangs'). The whole expression provides 'a remarkable mixed metaphor, in which death is regarded as being in labour and unable to hold back its child, the Messiah.'[12]

David's prophecy of the Messiah's triumph

As the prophecy of Joel was used to interpret and explain the gift of the Spirit in vv. 16–21, so now a second Old Testament citation is drawn into Peter's argument, to prepare for the claim that Jesus is the Christ (v. 36). Psalm 16 (LXX 15):8–11 is not quoted to 'prove' the resurrection as a historical event – the apostles

---

[12] W. Bauer, W.F. Arndt, F.W. Gingrich and F.W. Danker, *A Greek-English Lexicon of the New Testament and Other Early Christian Literature* (Chicago/London: University of Chicago Press, 1979², from Bauer's German original 1958⁵) (Henceforth: BAGD), 483f. Cf. G. Bertram, in *TDNT* IX, 673. The expression 'pangs of death' is found in Ps. 18:4 (LXX 17:5); 116 (LXX 114):3 and the parallel expression 'pangs of Hades' in Ps. 18:5 (LXX 17:6).

present themselves as witnesses in that particular respect (v. 32)
– but to show how the resurrection testifies to Jesus'
messiahship. It was impossible for death to keep its hold on
Jesus because of what *David* said about him (vv. 25–31).[13] Note
the use of the same passage in connection with Paul's preaching
about the resurrection to another audience of Jews and
proselytes in 13:34–7.

Psalm 16 celebrates the benefits of a life lived under the rule
of God. But David's joy reaches beyond his present
circumstances to include the hope that he will always be with
God (vv. 9–10; Acts 2:26–7). Death no longer terrifies him and he
affirms: 'you will not abandon my soul to Hades' (the Greek
word for the Hebrew Sheol), or let your Holy One experience
corruption.' The impotence of death to destroy his relationship
with God is David's confidence.[14] Since God has already made
known to him the paths of life, he anticipates that God will
continue to fill him with joy in his presence (v. 11; Acts 2:28). The
last clause of Psalm 16:11 ('in your right hand are pleasures for
evermore') is not quoted in Peter's sermon. But the implications
of Jesus' presence 'at God's right hand' are soon discussed in
relation to another psalm citation in vv. 33–4.

What elements in Psalm 16 lead to the understanding that it is
about the bodily resurrection of Jesus? In what sense could
David have spoken *about him* (lit. 'with reference to him', *eis
auton*)? The fact that the patriarch David 'died and was buried,
and his tomb is with us to this day', is sufficient proof for Peter
that Psalm 16 speaks about something beyond David's personal
experience.[15] Bodily resurrection is the key issue in his
understanding of this passage. If David's own body had been
raised, his grave would have been disturbed or would no longer
be present.

---

[13] Davidic authorship is affirmed by both the Hebrew and Greek versions of
this psalm and is clearly foundational to the argument here (cf. 1:20; 2:34–5).
[14] Cf. W. Eichrodt, *Theology of the Old Testament* (ET, London: SCM, 1967),
vol. 2, 524–5; D.L. Bock, *Proclamation from Prophecy and Pattern. Lucan Old
Testament Christology* (JSNTSS 12; Sheffield: JSOT, 1987), 173–4.
[15] David's tomb was situated on the slope of Ophel near the Pool of Siloam (cf.
Neh. 3:16). It was entered and robbed during the seige of Jerusalem in 135/134
BC. Over a century later Herod the Great built a monument of white marble at
its entrance (cf. Josephus, *Jewish War*, 1.61; *Antiquities* 7.393; 13.249;
16.179–83).

Peter's second assumption is that David was *a prophet*. This is implicit in what is said in 1:16 and 4:25 and was a common theme in Palestinian Judaism.[16] Jesus himself suggested the prophetic status of David when he gave a messianic interpretation of Psalm 110:1 (cf. Lk. 20:41–4 par.). Since that passage is paired with Psalm 16:8–11 in Acts 2:24–36, it is likely that Jesus' interpretation of Psalm 110 was the basis for the messianic reading of Psalm 16. Allusion is also made to another important Davidic psalm in v. 30 (cf. the use of Is. 55:3 LXX in Acts 13:34). David knew that 'God had sworn with an oath to him that he would put one of his descendants on his throne' (Ps. 132:11; cf. 2 Sam. 7:12–16; Ps. 89:3–4, 35–7). But how would this happen? Would it be by one descendant of David after another occupying the throne in Jerusalem? After the Babylonian Exile of the sixth century BC there were no more Davidic kings. How would God's covenant with David be maintained?

Peter insists that David was able to see what was ahead and speak of the resurrection of the Christ. Peter's point is that only through *resurrection from the dead* could a son of David rule for ever over God's people. David's confidence about his own resurrection was an oracular statement, inspired by the Spirit of God. It enabled him to indicate many centuries beforehand how God's covenant with him would ultimately be fulfilled. When Psalm 16:10 is cited again in v. 31, two significant changes are made. The past tense is employed to emphasize fulfilment – 'he was not abandoned to Hades, nor did his flesh experience corruption' – and 'his flesh' is substituted for 'your Holy One' (cf. v. 27). This last change 'guarantees that the point of the passage is not merely spiritual translation, bodily preservation, or terminal illness, but bodily resurrection.'[17]

So the Holy One is saved from death *in his flesh*. But who is this 'Holy One'? Most likely, the title 'your Holy One' was taken

---

[16] Cf. J.A. Fitzmyer, 'David, Being Therefore a Prophet . . .(Acts 2:30)', *Catholic Biblical Quarterly* 34 (1972), 332–9. It is surprising that Fitzmyer makes little of 2 Sam. 23:1–2 as an OT precedent.

[17] Bock, *Proclamation from Prophecy*, 178. This change reflects the explanatory parallelism of the Psalm as recorded in Acts 2:26b, 27, where 'the last two elements of the line define how the flesh shall dwell in security with hope' (v. 26, NIV *my body*).

by the earliest Christians to be another way of referring to the
Messiah and is a key for understanding Peter's use of this text.
Peter specifically links the hope of the psalmist with Jesus and
his resurrection. God has raised *this Jesus* to life (cf. v. 24) and
the apostles are all witnesses of the fact (cf. 1:8, 21–2). By
implication, he is the Christ. But that declaration is held over
until the dramatic climax of the message in v. 36.

What emerges in Acts 2, therefore, is the use of Jesus'
resurrection as part of an apologetic to Jews, based on a
distinctive way of looking at Scripture, apparently derived from
Jesus himself. This approach to the resurrection is reflected in
varying degrees in later addresses to Jewish audiences in Acts.
The resurrection demonstrates that Jesus is the Christ, who
fulfils a complex of Jewish hopes (cf. 3:15, 26; 4:10–12; 5:30–2;
10:40–3; 13:30–9). He is the saviour-king of David's line, who
reigns for ever over God's people, bringing the blessings of
forgiveness and peace with God. As the one appointed to be the
judge of the living and the dead, he offers salvation and a share
in his resurrection life to all nations (cf. 13:46–8; 16:30–1).

Gentile readers were perhaps meant to discern from this
Davidic emphasis that Christianity is the rightful heir of Old
Testament promises and that salvation comes through being
grafted into the vine of the renewed Israel. Acts goes on to show,
however, that even outright pagans were confronted with
aspects of this teaching about the resurrected Messiah/king,
adapted to their understanding and situation (cf. Thessalonica
(17:7, in the light of 17:1–3), and Athens (17:18, 30–1)).
Contemporary preachers of the gospel have something to learn
here. The resurrection does not simply prove Jesus' divinity but
inaugurates the End time of prophetic expectation, a new world
with the exalted Christ at its centre. The resurrection is also the
key to a complex and comprehensive offer of salvation.

The heavenly rule of the Messiah

The two themes of the sermon so far – an explanation of the gift
of the Spirit (vv. 16–21) and a proclamation of Jesus as Lord and
Christ (vv. 22–32) – are tied together in vv. 33–6. As a sequel to
his resurrection, Jesus was 'exalted at the right hand of God.'
From Psalm 110:1 it is demonstrated that this is the proper place
for the Messiah (vv. 34–5). Furthermore, Joel's prophecy has

been fulfilled by the resurrected and ascended Jesus. What the crowd at Pentecost could 'see and hear' were signs of Jesus' exaltation to the situation of absolute glory, power and authority in the universe. As the dispenser of the Spirit, he was now acting for the Father, sharing fully in his heavenly rule as Lord. With such teaching, the raw materials were provided for later formulations of the doctrine of God as Trinity.

Jesus' interpretation of Psalm 110:1 suggested that the enthronement of the Christ at God's right hand was a transcendental event (cf. Lk. 22:67–9 par.).[18] The apostles proclaimed his resurrection-ascension as the fulfilment of those expectations. By this means his heavenly rule as the saviour-king of his people was inaugurated. Resurrection and ascension belong together in Christian theology and proclamation, but not in a way that diminishes the significance of the resurrection as the means by which the Messiah himself was actually delivered from the power of death.

An indication that the sermon has reached its climax is given by Peter's address to all Israel again in v. 36, recalling v. 14. The link word 'therefore' also shows that he intends to summarize and conclude the argument of the preceding section. Peter's audience and subsequent readers of Acts are to be assured about who Jesus is and how God has vindicated him (cf. Lk. 1:4): 'God has made him both Lord and Messiah, this Jesus whom you crucified.' The two titles given to Jesus relate back to the psalm citations in vv. 25–34 and the prior claim of Joel 2:32 that whoever calls on the name of 'the Lord' will be saved (v. 21). Jesus is the Lord on whom to call, since he is the Messiah, resurrected by God in fulfilment of Psalm 16:8–11 and now exalted to his right hand in fulfilment of Psalm 110:1.[19]

---

[18] Cf. D.M. Hay, *Glory at the Right Hand. Psalm 110 in Early Christianity* (SBLMS 18; Nashville/New York: SBL, 1973), 110–16; Bock, *Proclamation from Prophecy*, 128–32. In the final analysis, Luke shows that 'the Messiah Jesus is not merely the Son of David or the messianic Son of God. He is Son in a fuller sense that entails complete authority and direct access to God' (Bock, 143).

[19] Ps. 2:7 is used instead of Ps. 110:1 in Acts 13:33, in conjunction with Ps. 16:10, in a similar apologetic. Since Ps. 2:7 puts the focus on Jesus as the exalted messianic Son, it is clear that 'Son of God' ((8:37); 9:20) conveys the same sense as 'Lord and Messiah' (2:36).

When Peter says God has made Jesus Lord and Messiah, we may not conclude that this is evidence of 'adoptionism', the view that Jesus was merely adopted as God's heavenly co-regent at this point in time. Jesus is proclaimed as Saviour, Messiah and Lord at his birth (Lk. 2:11; cf. 1:32–5; 3:22) and progressively demonstrates his identity in various ways throughout his earthly ministry. Because he was Messiah, Jesus was raised from death and exalted to God's right hand! However, just as there are several important stages in the life of a king, from birth as heir to the throne, to anointing, to actual assumption of his throne, so it is with Jesus in Luke–Acts.

> Although Jesus was called Lord and Messiah previously, the full authority of these titles is granted only through death, resurrection and exaltation. Peter's concluding statement in 2:36 makes it clear that something new and important has happened through these events. Jesus has been enthroned as Lord and Messiah for Israel, to fulfill all the promises made to it. This newly enthroned ruler will also offer salvation to the world, having been granted universal power to rule and judge.[20]

5. Jesus' resurrection inaugurates the new creation

Peter's address in Acts 3:11–26 proclaims the significance of the healing miracle in the first part of the chapter, identifying Jesus as the one who heals in the ultimate sense, fulfilling all that the Scriptures say about the Christ. The audience is challenged to repent and turn to God for forgiveness, especially acknowledging their part in the death of Jesus. As Peter speaks of Christ bringing about the promised restoration of all things, it becomes clear that the physical healing of the lame man is a sign of the messianic salvation in all its dimensions (cf. 4:9–12). It anticipates the new creation expected by the prophets, where there will be no evil, suffering, sickness or death. Moreover, this passage reveals how further strands of Luke's christology are linked with the theme of Jesus' resurrection.

---

[20] Tannehill, *Narrative Unity*, 39. R.N. Longenecker also argues that Peter is proclaiming 'not an adoptionist Christology but a functional one with ontological overtones' ('The Acts of the Apostles', *The Expositor's Bible Commentary*, (ed. F. E. Gaebelein; (Grand Rapids: Zondervan, 1981), vol. 9 281).

The glorification of the Servant of the Lord

God is said to have 'glorified his servant Jesus' (*edoxasen ton paida autou Iēsoun*) after he was dishonoured by those who handed him over to be killed and disowned him before Pilate (3:13). This appears to be an allusion to Isaiah 52:13 (LXX, *ho pais mou . . . doxasthesetai sphodra*, 'my servant will be highly exalted'), a verse which introduces the so-called 'Fourth Servant Song' in Isaiah 52:13–53:12. The glorification of the servant refers to his exaltation over the nations and their kings, after terrible humiliation and suffering.

An identification of Jesus as God's *servant* is found elsewhere in Acts (3:26; 4:27, 30). The title is more than a formal, honorific way of describing Jesus as a faithful follower or child of God.[21] Peter's sermon goes on to describe Jesus' rejection, death and exaltation by God (vv. 13–15) in a way that mirrors the portrait of the servant in Isaiah 53. When Peter insists that God has fulfilled what the prophets said about the suffering of *his Christ* (v. 18), it is logical to conclude that Isaiah 53 is a key text in his thinking. Jesus is the messianic servant who accomplished God's saving purposes for Israel and the nations by fulfilling the pattern set out in that Isaianic prophecy. The link between Isaiah 53 and the experience of Jesus is further established by the argument in Acts 8:32–5 (cf. Lk. 22:37).[22]

---

[21] E. Haenchen (*The Acts of the Apostles. A Commentary* (ET; Oxford: Blackwell, 1971), 205) takes 'servant' as a term adopted from Jewish prayers, 'in which great men of God, especially David, were called God's *pais'* (cf. Acts 4:25). D.L. Jones ('The Title "Servant" in Luke–Acts', in Talbert, C.H. (ed.), *Luke–Acts. New Perspectives from the Society of Biblical Literature Seminar* (New York: Crossroad, 1984), 148–65) develops this argument, concluding that Luke used the title 'servant' interchangeably with 'Son of God' and 'Christ', without any identification of Jesus as the Suffering Servant. It is true that two of the references to Jesus as God's servant in Acts are in the context of prayer (4:27, 30) and that the title mainly lived on as a fixed liturgical formula in some later Christian works, without necessarily connoting his vicarious suffering. But the usage in Acts 3:13, 26 is in an explanatory and apologetic context, with Isaianic associations clearly established in the intervening argument. Cf. Barrett, *Acts*, vol. 1, 194.

[22] Further links with Isa. 53 have been detected in Luke's passion narrative; see P.M. Head, 'The Self-Offering and Death of Christ as a Sacrifice in the Gospels and the Acts of the Apostles' in R.T. Beckwith and M. Selman (eds), *Sacrifice in the Bible* (Carlisle: Paternoster/Grand Rapids: Baker, 1995), 111–29, n. 52, 127.

Jesus was glorified by his resurrection and subsequent exaltation into heaven (vv. 14–16). However, it should not be forgotten that Peter's sermon began as an explanation of the healing of the crippled man (v. 12) and that the apostle soon identifies Jesus as the power behind this miracle (v. 16). It seems best, therefore, to suggest that Jesus' glorification may have a double meaning in this context: Jesus is glorified by his heavenly exaltation and by the exercise of his continuing, heavenly authority in a healing like this.[23]

The raising of the Author of life

As in 2:23, 36, the Jerusalemites are directly charged with repudiating Jesus (cf. 4:10; 5:30; 7:52; 13:28), but the theme of rejection is much more prominent in 3:13–15 than in Peter's first sermon. In v. 15 they are even charged with killing 'the author of life.' The term *archēgos* in Greek literature and the papyri hovers between the two senses of 'leader, prince' and 'author, originator.'[24] In 5:31 this noun is used in conjunction with the title 'Saviour', in an expression which English versions render 'Prince and Saviour' or 'Leader and Saviour.' In 3:15 the translation 'Prince of life' (AV, JBP) is similarly possible, since Jesus by his resurrection has become the one who has 'led the way to life' (NEB). However, the full import of the construction is better conveyed by the translation *author of life* (NRSV, NIV). By virtue of his death and resurrection, Jesus is the originator of new life for others, as the argument in vv. 16–21 goes on to suggest.

In simple terms it was the exalted Lord Jesus who healed the crippled beggar. But the 'name' of Jesus continues to be the focus of Peter's thinking in 3:16 because he knows that the salvation promised by Joel and other eschatological prophets

---

[23] Cf. Bock, *Proclamation from Prophecy*, 189–90; Tannehill, *Narrative Unity*, 53. Jesus' exaltation is testified to by this healing just as it is testified to by the pouring out of the Holy Spirit (2:33–6).

[24] Cf. P.G. Müller, ΧΡΙΣΤΟΣ ΑΡΧΗΓΟΣ: *Der religionsgeschichtliche und theologische Hintergrund einer neutestamentlichen Christusprädikation* (Europäische Hochsculschriften Reihe 23, Frankfurt/Bern: Lang, 1973), vol. 28; 1–247; G. Johnston, 'Christ as Archegos', *New Testament Studies* 27 (1981), 381–5.

(cf. Joel 2:32 in Acts 2:21) is for those who call upon the name of Jesus Christ (cf. Acts 2:38). The healing of this crippled man is a pointer to the saving power of Jesus in the widest sense (cf. 4:10–12).

Experiencing the benefits of Christ's death and resurrection

Having made a series of powerful accusations against his contemporaries (vv. 13–15), Peter challenges them to repent and turn to God (v. 19). Repentance is demanded on the basis of what has been proclaimed about Jesus' suffering and exaltation (3:16–18). Three positive encouragements to repent are then given in a series of purpose clauses. The first is 'so that your sins may be wiped out' (v. 19), and the second is 'so that times of refreshing may come from the presence of the Lord' (v. 20). Some have argued that this last expression refers to the messianic salvation in all its fullness, which God will send speedily if Israel repents.[25] This involves taking the next clause ('that he may send the Messiah appointed for you') as a complementary statement about the same event. However, vv. 20–1 suggest a sequence, by which these *times* (*kairoi*, plural) of refreshment occur in an intervening period, before Christ's return and the consummation of God's plan. Even now, those who turn to him for forgiveness may enjoy in advance some of the blessings associated with the coming era.[26] A comparison with Peter's promises in 2:38 suggests that the Holy Spirit may be the one who brings this refreshment. Peter may be describing the subjective effect of the gift of the Spirit for believers at significant stages in their lives.

The apostle finally urges repentance so that God may 'send the Messiah appointed for you, that is, Jesus.' There is no specific

---

[25] E.g. Haenchen, *Acts*, 208 n. 8; E. Schweizer in *TDNT* IX, 663–5. The verb *anapsychein* basically means 'to cool, refresh' (e.g. Jdg. 15:19; 2 Sam. 16:14; 2 Macc. 4:46 LXX; 2 Tim. 1:16). The sense of relief from suffering is prominent in Ps. 38:14 (LXX).

[26] Perhaps these times of refreshment are more specifically 'moments of relief during the time men spend in waiting for that blessed day' (C.K. Barrett, 'Faith and Eschatology in Acts 3' in E. Grässer, and O. Merk (eds.), *Glaube und Eschatologie: Festschrift für W.G. Kümmel* (Tübingen: Mohr, 1985), 12). Barrett suggests that we have here 'an example of Luke's personalizing, or individualizing, of eschatology' (12f.).

mention of Jesus' second coming elsewhere in the apostolic preaching, though Jesus' role as 'judge of the living and the dead' is highlighted (10:42; cf. 7:55–6; 17:31). Jesus was the one 'accredited' (2:22, *apodedeigmenon*) by God to Israel in the course of his earthly ministry. He suffered as 'the Christ' (3:18), but by means of his resurrection and ascension, became the heavenly, enthroned ruler envisaged in Psalm 110 (cf. 2:36). Peter's point in 3:19–20 is that the previously rejected Messiah will only return if Israel repents.

The second coming of Jesus is not represented as an occasion for judgement here. Rather, he must 'remain in heaven' (lit. 'whom heaven must receive') 'until the time of universal restoration that God announced long ago through his holy prophets.' Jesus' present withdrawal from the earthly scene is an important stage in the divine plan of salvation. His withdrawal will continue (lit.) 'until the times of restoration of all things', when 'God, through Christ, will restore his fallen world to the purity and integrity of its initial creation.'[27] NIV implies that this will take place when Christ returns. But the Greek could just as easily mean that a process of restoration is already underway (note the use of the plural 'times') and that Jesus' return will mark its climax and dramatic conclusion.

The restoration of 'the kingdom' to Israel is probably meant to be understood as part of this process (cf. 1:6, where the cognate verb *apokathistēmi* is used). Acts 2 suggests that the restoration of Israel began with the preaching of the gospel and the pouring out of God's Spirit. Acts 3 illustrates that restoration with the healing of the crippled man. However, this miracle also anticipates the ultimate renewal of the whole created order, as God announced long ago 'through his holy prophets' (e.g., Isa. 35:1–10; 65:17–25; Ezek. 47:1–12; cf. Rom. 8:18–23; 2 Pet. 3:10–13; Rev. 21:1–7; 22:1–5). Furthermore, Peter goes on to teach that the blessing of all the peoples on earth through the messianic restoration of Israel must first take place (Acts 3:25–6; cf. 1:7–8).

In other words, the restoration of all things has begun and will continue until it is consummated at Christ's return. But 'the times of universal restoration' and 'times of refreshing' (v. 19)

---

[27] Barrett, 'Faith and Eschatology', 16.

are not simply synonymous or interchangeable terms.[28] 'Consistent with his eschatological scenario sketched in Luke 21:5–36, Luke separates the time of witness from the end-time.' [29] Yet there is also a sense in which he proclaims the realization of end-time blessings in the present through the preaching of the gospel and the healing that accompanies it.

6. Jesus as the fulfilment of Israel's resurrection hope

In Acts 2 – 3, the resurrection is intimately connected with the suffering of Jesus and his subsequent ascension and heavenly enthronement. The salvation and restoration proclaimed in the apostolic gospel is made possible by this complex of events. Nevertheless, the resurrection receives special prominence as the event that inaugurates the eschatological process. This perspective is confirmed in Acts 4, where Luke notes that the priests, the captain of the temple and the Sadducees were annoyed because the apostles were 'teaching the people and proclaiming that in Jesus there is the resurrection of the dead' (v. 2).

Sadducees and Christians

The Sadducean party, which was made up of chief priests and elders, the priestly and the lay nobility, denied that on the last day there would be a general resurrection from the dead (cf. Lk.

---

[28] A. Oepke, in *TDNT*, I, p. 391, suggests that *anapsyxeōs* ('refreshment, relief') denotes the subjective side of what God is doing in the present and that *apokatastaseōs* ('restoration, reconstitution') denotes the objective side of the matter (the restoration of right relationships and the reconstitution of the creation). However, I am not convinced by his distinction between the two different words for 'times', *kairoi* (marking 'the beginning of the transformation') and *chronōn* (conveying 'the thought of the lasting nature of the renewed world'). Cf. Barrett, 'Faith and Eschatology', 10–11.

[29] L.T. Johnson, *The Acts of the Apostles* (Sacra Pagina 5; Collegeville: Liturgical Press, 1992), 74. Cf. W. Kurz, 'Acts 3:19–26 as a Test of the Role of Eschatology in Lukan Christology' in P.J. Achtemeier (ed.), *SBL 1977 Seminar Papers* (Missoula: Scholars, 1977), 309–23.

20:27; Acts 23:7–8).[30] They regarded the Maccabean heroes,
Mattathias, Judas, Jonathan, and Simon (164–134 BC) as having
inaugurated the Messianic Age (cf. Jub. 23:23–34; 31:9–20;
1 Macc. 14:4–15, 41). 'For them, the Messiah was an ideal, not a
person, and the Messianic Age was a process, not a cataclysmic
or even datable event.' [31]

The Sadducees as a party had no specific authority in the
temple but many of the priests came from their ranks. They were
offended because the apostles as 'uneducated and ordinary men'
(4:13) were teaching the people in the precincts of the temple.
What disturbed them most, however, was that the apostles were
affirming what the Sadducees expressly denied, proclaiming in
Jesus the resurrection from the dead. The expression 'in Jesus'
(*en tō Iēsou*) probably means 'in the case of Jesus.' They were
affirming the prophetic hope for a general resurrection by
means of the story of Jesus. But they were also making it clear
that his resurrection is the key to the fulfilment of that hope. As
the flow of the argument in Acts 3–4 suggests, it is because of
Jesus' resurrection that God's promise to 'restore everything'
(3:21) will most surely be accomplished and those who trust in
Jesus will enjoy all the benefits of the salvation that his
resurrection makes possible (4:10–12).

Salvation 'by the name of Jesus Christ'

The 'name' of Jesus, which was given some prominence in 2:38;
3:6, 16, continues to be a dominant theme in chapter four (vv. 7,
10, 12, 17, 18, 30). Peter and John are tried by the Sanhedrin in
connection with the healing of the lame man in the temple
forecourt and the preaching about Jesus that ensued. The main
concern of the authorities is: 'by what power or by what name
did you do this?'

In Peter's response, the Greek word *sōzō* is used in two
different ways. It refers firstly to healing in a physical sense (v. 9,

---

[30] On the Sadducean beliefs, cf. Josephus, *Antiquities*, 13:297–8; 18:16–17;
Jewish War, 2:164–5; and E.M. Schürer (rev. and ed. by G. Vermes, F. Millar and
M. Black), *The History of the Jewish People in the Age of Jesus Christ (175 BC –
AD 135)* (Edinburgh: T.&T. Clark, 1973–87), vol. 2, 404–14.

[31] Longenecker, 'Acts', 301. He notes the link between their political views and
their eschatology.

cf. *therapeuō* in v. 14). It is then used in v. 12, together with the noun *sōtēria*, to refer to salvation in the sense outlined in Peter's Pentecost sermon, namely, rescue from the coming judgement of God and enjoyment of life under God's rule in the messianic age (2:21, 40, 47). As in 2:22–36 and 3:13–18, Peter argues that God has accomplished his eschatological purpose through the death and resurrection of Jesus. In raising him from the dead, God began the great process of renewal and restoration that will culminate in a transformed creation and the resurrection to eternal life (3:19–21). What happened to the crippled man was an anticipation of the glory to come but also a sign of the present, heavenly authority of the exalted Christ.

In terms of Psalm 118:22 (LXX 117:22), Jesus is the despised 'stone', rejected by the leaders of Israel, but exalted by God to the place of highest honour and significance. He is now 'the cornerstone' (lit. 'head of a corner'), playing a critical role in the building which God is constructing.[32] In other words, he is the key figure in God's plan for the restoration of Israel and the whole of his creation. In the original context of the psalm, the stone is either Israel or Israel's king, rejected by the nations but chosen by God for the accomplishment of his purpose. As elsewhere in the New Testament, however, 'God's purpose for Israel finds its fulfilment in the single-handed work of the Christ.'[33] Israel's destiny is tied up with what happens to its king.

The centrality of Jesus to God's purpose is stressed again with the assertion that 'there is salvation in no one else' (v. 12). This is so because 'there is no other name under heaven given among mortals by which we must be saved.' Jesus' name is 'the inescapable decision point concerning salvation.'[34] Members of the Sanhedrin would doubtless have agreed that Israel's God was the only saviour (cf. Isa. 43:11–12; 45:22). But Peter's point is that, even for Israel, the name of Jesus is now the only means by which God's saving power can be invoked and experienced.

---

[32] Longenecker ('Acts', 304–5) notes that in the first century AD *Testament of Solomon* 22:7–23:4 'the stone at the head of the corner' unambiguously refers to 'the final copestone or capstone placed on the summit of the Jerusalem temple to complete the whole edifice'. Cf. J. Jeremias, in *TDNT*, I, 792.

[33] F.F. Bruce, *The Book of the Acts, Revised Edition* (NICNT; Grand Rapids: Eerdmans, 1988), 93.

[34] Tannehill, *Narrative Unity*, 61.

There is a divine necessity (*dei*) about calling upon the name that God has provided, because of Jesus' unique place in the divine plan (v. 11). And it is the resurrection that establishes him as 'the cornerstone' in this context, after his rejection by 'the builders.'

It is difficult for people in a relativistic, multifaith society to accept the exclusive claim of Acts 4:12. Various alternatives have been proposed to weaken its impact, including the notion that Jesus somehow benefits sincere adherents of other religions, even though they do not acknowledge him as Saviour and Lord. But such an approach is not consistent with the teaching of Acts 2 – 3, that it is actually necessary to *call* upon the name of Jesus to benefit from the salvation he offers (cf. Paul's use of Joel 2:32 in Rom. 10:12–15).

Christians and Pharisees

In the concluding chapters of the book of Acts, when Paul makes his defence in a variety of contexts, he identifies himself with the position of the Pharisees. The name 'Pharisee' probably derives from the Aramaic verb 'to separate.' The Pharisees saw themselves as 'the separated' or 'the holy ones', who kept aloof from those who were casual about keeping God's law. They were a continuation of the ancient Hasidim ('pious ones'), who joined the Hasmonaean rulers in their struggle for religious freedom in the time when the Seleucids controlled Palestine (second century BC). They withdrew their support, however, when the Hasmonaeans went on to establish political as well as military supremacy for themselves and assumed the high-priesthood.[35] The Pharisees came from diverse backgrounds to devote themselves to the study of the Law in its written and oral forms. They applied the Law to the contemporary scene, but also sought to prepare God's people for the coming of the Messianic Age by summoning them to live a holy life. In the first century AD, their influence in the Sanhedrin was gradually increasing.

Before that same council, Paul identified himself as 'a Pharisee, a son of Pharisees' and declared that he was on trial 'concerning the hope of the resurrection of the dead' (23:6). On this key matter, the Christian movement aligned itself with the

---

[35] Cf. Bruce, *The Book of the Acts*, 114f. n. 51; Schürer, *The History of the Jewish People* (rev.), vol. 2, 381–403.

Pharisees rather than the Sadducees concerning the future of Israel (23:8). Paul's appeal was not simply a political ploy to turn the members of the Sanhedrin against one another. He claimed to have views that were consistent with those of his teachers (cf. 22:3) and many on the council itself.

Although the Pharisees looked for the resurrection of the dead, there were diverse views in Jewish thought about whether that meant the resuscitation of the body or not.[36] Christian preaching clearly came down on the side of a physical resurrection and identified Jesus as the one in whom the hope of a general resurrection would be fulfilled. From an apologetic point of view, affirming the Pharisaic hope was a way of affirming the prophetic expectations that lay behind it. It was also the way to point those with such convictions to the significance of Jesus in the outworking of God's purposes.

There has been some scepticism amongst commentators about the reliability of Luke's presentation of Paul in these chapters. I do not wish to enter that debate at this point. But Haenchen is surely right to highlight Luke's intention to show that a fellowship between Pharisaism and Christianity is in the end possible:

> The Pharisees also hope for the Messiah, await the resurrection of the dead. In this they are at one with the Christians. Their mistake is only that in this hope and faith they are not consistent where Jesus is concerned. The resurrection of Jesus, and his Messiahship thereby attested, are not contrary to the Jewish faith.[37]

Putting it another way, Luke believed that the hope of the resurrection could be 'a shared starting point with some Jews.'[38] By way of contrast, pagans are pictured in Acts as reacting negatively to preaching about a bodily resurrection (17:32; 26:23–4).

---

[36] Cf. C. Brown, 'Resurrection' in *NIDNTT*, vol. 3, 270–5.

[37] Haenchen, *Acts*, 643. On the Jewishness of Paul that Luke brings out so obviously in Acts, cf. J. Jervell, 'Paul in the Acts of the Apostles' in J. Kremer (ed.), *Les Acts des Apôtres* (Leuven: Leuven University, 1979), 297–306.

[38] Tannehill, *Narrative Unity*, 288. Paul is presented in these chapters as 'a model of a resourceful missionary who takes account of the presuppositions of his audience' (289).

In Acts 24, responding to the accusations of his Jewish opponents before Felix the Roman governor, Paul again claims to be on trial concerning the resurrection from the dead (v. 21). He presents himself as an orthodox Jew, who worships 'the God of our ancestors, believing everything laid down according to the law or written in the prophets' (v. 15). His service to God, however, is 'according to the Way', which his opponents call 'a sect' (*hairesis*). Yet his apparently sectarian approach to Judaism has at its core a hope in God that 'there will be a resurrection of both the righteous and the unrighteous' (v. 15; cf. Dan. 12:2; Jn. 5:28–9; Rev. 20:12–15). This last expression links the thought of judgement with that of resurrection, as the next verse makes clear. It is because of the resurrection that Paul does his best to have 'a clear conscience toward God and all people' (v. 17).

Although Paul is opposed by the high priest Ananias 'with some elders and an attorney' (24:1), he boldly claims that his hope is one that 'they themselves also accept' (24:15). He ignores the presence of Sadducees amongst his accusers and insists that 'it was the Pharisaic hope that characterized – or, at least, should characterize – all true representations of the Jewish faith.'[39]

Paul's defence before Herod Agrippa II in Acts 26 is his most extensive, because he knows Agrippa to be especially familiar with 'all the customs and controversies of the Jews' (v. 3).[40] Once again he establishes himself as an orthodox Jew, who previously belonged to 'the strictest sect' of Judaism and who lived as a Pharisee (v. 5). Once again he claims to be on trial for his resurrection faith, describing it as a hope in 'the promise made by God to our ancestors, a promise that our twelve tribes hope to attain, as they earnestly worship day and night' (v. 6). In other words, the hope of Israel for a restoration of the twelve tribes, under a renewed covenant, in a renewed creation, is here focused on the expectation of a resurrection of the dead. Paul considers it incredible that he is accused by the Jews for proclaiming *this hope* (v. 7), which he later characterizes as 'the hope of Israel' (28:20).

---

[39] Longenecker, 'Acts', 540. K. Haacker ('Bekenntnis des Paulus zur Hoffnung Israels', *New Testament Studies* 31 (1985), 443–8) shows how the theme of resurrection is closely connected in the OT and Jewish tradition with the hopes of Israel as a people.

[40] Cf. R.F. O'Toole, *Acts 26 The Christological Climax of Paul's Defence (Acts 22:1 – 26:32)* (Analecta Biblica 78; Rome: Pontifical Biblical Institute, 1978).

In his former commitment to Judaism, Paul saw Jesus of Nazareth and his followers as opponents (26:9–12). Confronted by the risen Christ on the road to Damascus, his understanding of the way in which the hope of Israel would be fulfilled was dramatically changed (vv. 13–16). From then on, he continued to say 'nothing but what the prophets and Moses said would take place' (v. 22). But his encounter with Christ enabled him to discern 'that the Messiah must suffer, and that, by being the first to rise from the dead, he would proclaim light both to our people and to the Gentiles' (v. 23).

Summary: the appeal to Jewish audiences

Paul is pictured in the closing chapters of Acts as one who finds ways to speak even to hostile Jews, 'building a foundation for mutual understanding.'[41] Only in the case of King Agrippa, who is less hostile, does he get to the point of a full missionary appeal (26:27–9). Tannehill notes that Paul's approach to Jews in this respect is similar to his approach to pagans in Acts 17:

> In both cases Paul avoids reference to Jesus until a foundation has been laid, in one case through presenting a view of God that cultured pagans might accept, in the other case through emphasizing the hope that Paul and other Jews share. Such an approach is necessary because Paul is speaking to groups who are difficult to reach.[42]

Acts 26:23 provides an opportunity to summarize the way in which the suffering and resurrection of Jesus are used in Luke–Acts in appealing to Jewish audiences. The suffering of the Messiah inaugurates the New Covenant (Lk. 22:15–20), which makes possible the definitive offer of forgiveness that is at the heart of the apostolic preaching (Lk. 24:47; Acts 2:38; 5:31; 10:43; 13:38; 26:18). Jesus' sacrifice is thus the means by which God's new covenant people are constituted, in fulfilment of Jeremiah 31:31–4.[43] The resurrection is necessary, however, to free the Messiah himself from the power of death and make him 'the first to rise from the dead' in God's great plan of restoration

---

[41] Tannehill, *Narrative Unity*, 290.
[42] Tannehill, *Narrative Unity*, 290.
[43] For a brief survey of the scholarly debate regarding Luke's perspective on the death of Jesus see Head, 'The Self-Offering and Death of Christ', 116–19.

for Israel and the nations. The resurrection also makes possible his ascension and heavenly enthronement, so that he can pour out God's Spirit on his disciples and subdue the enemies of God, before the End comes (2:32–9).

Through the ministry of his Spirit-led people, he continues to 'proclaim light' to the people of Israel and also to the Gentiles, showing them the way to salvation through him. As the exalted Lord and Messiah, he has become the 'cornerstone' in the divine plan. There is no other 'name' to call upon to share in the blessings of the messianic era and the restoration of all things that will climax with his return.

7. Jesus' resurrection and the appeal to pagans

The account of Paul's ministry in Athens (Acts 17:16–34) gives some indication of the way the Christian message had to be preached to convince the pagan mind. This is anticipated in the much briefer record of Paul's preaching at Lystra (14:11–18). Luke first notes that, when Paul was waiting for his friends in Athens, 'he was deeply distressed to see that the city was full of idols' (17:16). His reaction was twofold. As was his custom, he turned first to the synagogue and reasoned with the Jews and God-fearing Greeks. Doubtless he preached Jesus as the Christ and showed how the Scriptures had been fulfilled in his death and resurrection (cf. 13:16–41; 17:2–4). However, he also dialogued in the marketplace daily with 'those who happened to be there.'

Jesus and the resurrection

Paul may well have employed some of the argument detailed later in the chapter, but those who heard him were convinced that his message was essentially about 'Jesus and the resurrection' (v. 18). In other words, Paul was not simply engaged in apologetics or pre-evangelism. He apparently saw that the preaching of Jesus and the resurrection was the key to persuading those who were given over to idolatry. For all that, some of his listeners categorized him as yet another preacher of 'foreign gods' or strange powers (v. 18).[44]

Such novel teaching had to be examined by the experts in the court of the Areopagus, an ancient institution exercising jurisdiction in religion and morals in Athens (vv. 19–20). Paul's defence in this context carefully weaves the themes of *ignorance* and *worship* together. He notes the extent of their religious feeling, as indicated by the many objects of their devotion (*sebasmata*), but insists that the altar dedicated 'to an unknown god' is a pointer to their ignorance of the true God (vv. 22–3).

Biblical foundations

When the text of the following verses is closely examined, it is clear that Paul puts forward a number of Old Testament perspectives about the character and purpose of God, the foolishness of idolatry, and human responsibility in relation to God, *without actually quoting scripture* (vv. 24–29).[45] The true God cannot be accommodated in human sanctuaries and have his needs met by those who would serve him. The God who made the world and everything in it, 'he who is Lord of heaven and earth, does not live in shrines made by human hands, nor is he served by human hands, as though he needed anything, since he himself gives to all mortals life and breath and all things' (vv. 24–5). Each part of this carefully worded statement attacks an important presupposition of paganism. Furthermore, God's ordering of nature and history is designed to provoke people to 'search for God and perhaps grope for him and find him' (vv. 26–7).

The characteristic response of humanity has been the lie of idolatry, even though it is totally illogical and has often been acknowledged as such by pagan poets and philosophers

---

[44] For a brief analysis of the Stoic and Epicurean philosophies and the reaction to Paul's message, see Bruce, *The Book of the Acts*, 330–1. When Paul spoke about 'Jesus and the resurrection' it is possible that they understood him to be speaking about 'the personified and divinized powers of "healing" and "restoration".'

[45] So argues Bruce, *The Book of the Acts*, 334–5, while defending the authenticity of this speech and discussing its relation to the theology of Romans 1 – 3. The essential context of the speech is biblical, 'but the presentation is Hellenistic' (341).

(vv. 28–9). Such 'ignorance' of God is actually culpable. In the framework of teaching about the judgement of God against all false worship, Paul then returns to the theme of Jesus and the resurrection (vv. 30–1).

The appeal for conversion

Tannehill rightly observes that effective mission requires reflection on theological foundations 'in order to discover a message that can address the whole world.'[46] Reflection on the relation of the Creator to the creation in Acts 17 enables Paul to proclaim a message that excludes no one. It arises from a profound understanding of the Jewish Scriptures but is taught in connection with ideas and practices manifested in the particular context addressed. Yet, although Paul seeks areas of common understanding with his audience, his speech is basically a call to repentance, 'a call for the Greco-Roman world to break decisively with its religious past in response to the one God who now invites all to be part of the renewed world.'[47]

Paul's conclusion is that Gentiles can seek after God and find him by turning in repentance from their idolatry and believing in the resurrected Jesus.[48] Even though the Creator has 'overlooked the times of ignorance', not acting in judgement as he might have in response to human sin, 'now he commands all people everywhere to repent' (v. 30). God will indeed act as judge and has already 'fixed a day on which he will have the world judged in righteousness' (v. 31). But perhaps the most surprising feature of this appeal is the statement that he will do this 'by a man whom he has appointed, and of this he has given assurance by raising him from the dead.'

The record of this address is brief and more was doubtless said by way of explanation on the day. Readers of Acts, however, have been prepared to understand the import of Paul's appeal from

---

[46] Tannehill, *Narrative Unity*, 211. Tannehill (211–12) also shows how the speech in Acts 17 repeats themes presented elsewhere in Luke–Acts.

[47] Tannehill, *Narrative Unity*, 218.

[48] On the preaching of the resurrected Christ as the centre of true worship for the nations, cf. R.F. O'Toole, 'Paul at Athens and Luke's notion of Worship', *Revue Biblique* 89 (1982), 185–97. However, his insistence that the speech is a 'Lukan literary work' needs to be weighed in the light of Bruce, *The Book of the Acts*, 334–42.

what has gone before. The resurrected Jesus is 'the one ordained by God as judge of the living and the dead' (10:41–2). This is so because of his exaltation to God's right hand, there to 'sit' until God makes his enemies his footstool (2:33–5). Everyone who responds to him with repentance and faith receives the forgiveness of sins and the gift of the Holy Spirit (2:38–9). Those who refuse him will be 'rooted out of the people' and find no place in the coming restoration (3:19–23).

The doctrine of the resurrection is not 'tagged on in a sudden transition in verse 31.'[49] Resurrection is critical to the argument because it is a 'proof' that the Creator God whom Paul represents is sovereign over nature and history, that he cannot be avoided and must in the end be judge of all. More particularly, it is a 'proof' of the significance of the man who was raised. The resurrection confirms the teaching about the importance of humanity in the divine plan set out in vv. 25–8. At the same time, it affirms that there is one man who is to be the standard and the agent of divine judgement for all.

Such preaching about the resurrection from the dead and the need to acknowledge the divine kingship of Jesus inevitably led the early Christians into direct conflict with the pluralism and relativism of the Greco-Roman world. 'When they heard of the resurrection of the dead, some scoffed; but others said, "We will hear you again about this"' (v. 32). Luke's final point, however, is that some believed (v. 33) and the implication is that the preaching of the resurrection of Jesus was the key to effective evangelism in a pagan, as well as in a Jewish context.

8. Conclusion

Contemporary apologists for Christianity operate in a very different context from the preachers in Acts. The closest parallel to our situation is Paul's encounter with paganism in Acts 17. In modern western culture, few have any knowledge of the biblical background assumed in the apostolic preaching to Jews. But those who wish to communicate the gospel to our own generation would do well to recover and apply those same perspectives, even as Paul does embryonically in Acts 17.

---

[49] Haenchen, *Acts*, 530.

The sermons in Acts highlight the theological issues that rightly belong with the proclamation of the resurrection of Jesus. They show that the resurrection links together a whole complex of biblical hopes and is a key to their fulfilment. Proclaimed within that framework, even in a summary way to pagans, the resurrection makes a powerful appeal to acknowledge the significance of Christ in the plan of God for humanity and the whole created order.

Jesus' resurrection affirms God's intention to judge humanity, but also to renew and transform all who call upon the name of Christ and, with them, the whole creation. It is a guarantee of the ultimate defeat of sin and all its consequences. It is a pointer to the supreme authority and significance of Jesus Christ for the whole human race. It makes him the living Lord, to whom all are accountable, the measure and standard of God's righteousness, but one from whom forgiveness and the gift of the Holy Spirit are available. It is the risen Lord who makes available 'times of refreshing', in anticipation of 'the universal restoration that God announced long ago through his holy prophets.'

Questions for further study

1. From your reading of Acts consider how adequate it is to say that the resurrection proves that Jesus is the Son of God.

2. How was the resurrection of Jesus the means by which 'the hope of Israel' was fulfilled?

3. How is the message to Israel about Jesus adapted for Gentile audiences in the Acts of the Apostles? What gets left out and what gets proclaimed in a new way?

4. Reflecting on Acts, to what extent would you say that teaching about the resurrection of Jesus is vital for persuading unbelievers today?

5. How would you answer the charge that the resurrection in Luke–Acts is only a stage in Jesus' heavenly exaltation and that Luke's real interest is in the ascension and enthronement of Christ? What is the distinctive importance of the resurrection in Luke's theology?

Select Bibliography

Bock, D.L., *Proclamation from Prophecy and Pattern. Lucan Old Testament Christology* (JSNTSS 12; Sheffield: JSOT, 1987)

Marshall, I.H., 'The Resurrection in the Acts of the Apostles' in W.W. Gasque, and R.P. Martin (eds.), *Apostolic History and the Gospel Biblical and historical Essays presented to F.F. Bruce on his 60th Birthday* (Exeter: Paternoster, 1970), 92–107

O'Toole, R.F., 'Luke's understanding of Jesus' resurrection-ascension-exaltation', *Biblical Theology Bulletin* 9 (1979), 106–14

Tannehill, R.C., *The Narrative Unity of Luke–Acts: A Literary Interpretation, Volume 2 The Acts of the Apostles* (Minneapolis: Fortress, 1990)

Three

Jesus' Resurrection in Pauline Thought: A Study in the Epistle to the Romans

PETER HEAD

1. Introduction

The resurrection of Jesus of Nazareth, who came to be known as Jesus Christ, is both foundational and central to the thought of Saul of Tarsus, who came to be known as the apostle Paul. Indeed, I speak in this way of these two men precisely because historically speaking it was *the resurrection itself* which resulted both in Jesus being recognized as the Messiah by his disciples and in the call and commission of Paul to be apostle to the Gentiles. Indeed, one of my primary concerns in what follows will be to highlight the fundamental connection in Paul's thought between that resurrection of Jesus as Messiah and Paul's own apostolic mission to the Gentiles, particularly as expressed in his letter to the Christians in Rome. This concentration is necessary because the resurrection of Jesus Christ is *so* central to the thought of the apostle Paul that we could not hope to cover the whole of Paul's thought in relation to the resurrection within the scope of the time or space available. Not only is the resurrection of Jesus mentioned in all but three of the Pauline epistles (2 Thess., Tit., Philem.), it is also discussed explicitly in a number of passages on a number of subjects, with a special role in Paul's ethics and eschatology; and dealt with at length in the longest chapter in his epistles (1 Cor. 15). Rather than focusing on a single theme or passage we shall be investigating the role of Jesus' resurrection in Paul's epistle to the Romans. This concentration could be justified in a number of ways.

First, even if we can no longer regard Romans as a compendium of Christian doctrine in a systematic sense (after Melanchthon), it remains the case that in this epistle Paul spells out the logic of the gospel at considerable length precisely in order to persuade a church in which he has never ministered to support the ministry of that gospel in regions west of Rome. No doubt (with Wedderburn) the peculiar and specific situation in Rome did influence the overall argument and content of the epistle, but one aspect of that situation – the hearers' ignorance of Paul and his gospel – forces him to spell out his teaching at greater length than in any other letter (as Cranfield insists).[1]

Second, arising out of the point just made and enforced no doubt by its canonical primacy, Romans has functioned in the history of Protestant thought mainly as a resource for reformation in which justification by faith has been central. This has placed justification and atonement at the forefront of the interpretation and utilization of Romans, especially for evangelical writers and preachers. A reading of Romans which pays special attention to the resurrection of Jesus may serve to highlight other themes of Romans which have perhaps played less prominent roles in evangelical thought.

Third, although it is not my intention to focus on questions about the historicity and reality of Jesus' resurrection, it is possible that a study of Romans may make some tangential contribution to the perennial debates on this matter. Indeed, precisely because, unlike for example in 1 Corinthians where the resurrection is a matter of dispute and direct instruction,

---

[1] A.J.M. Wedderburn, *The Reasons for Romans* (Edinburgh: T.&T. Clark, 1991); C.E.B. Cranfield, *A Critical and Exegetical Commentary on the Epistle to the Romans* (2 vols.; ICC; Edinburgh: T.&T. Clark, 1975, 1979), vol. 2, 814–22. Cranfield argued that 'the inner logic of the gospel' determined the structure and content of the letter (p. 818; cf. also D.J. Moo, who often uses the same language in *The Epistle to the Romans* (NICNT; Grand Rapids: Eerdmans, 1996), e.g. 20).

Romans may offer (and indeed, in my view does offer) considerable support for the view that the resurrection of Jesus is at the absolute heart of Pauline Christianity and that this centrality could be assumed when writing to a (previously) non-Pauline Christian group in Rome.

Fourth, it will shortly become clear that taking Romans as a whole, many fundamental aspects of Paul's thought *are* addressed in relation to the resurrection (e.g. christology, apostleship, justification, the Christian life and future hope). In this way Romans can function as a window onto other aspects of Paul's thought. In addition, while the general subject of the resurrection in Pauline thought has been given considerable treatment in the scholarly literature, there is very little which deals explicitly with its place in the argument of Romans.[2] Furthermore, I plan to make a strong new argument emphasising the important place which Jesus' resurrection occupies in Paul's appeal to the Roman Christians. In fact, the core of the argument I shall be trying to make is precisely *that it is the resurrection of the Messiah which is at the heart of Paul's vision of the gospel and his appeal to the Roman Christians.*

This paper begins with Paul in Romans 1 and deals with Jesus' resurrection and Paul's gospel and apostleship (section II) and then moves directly to his concluding appeal in 15:7-13. This establishes both the main framework and the heart of the argument: the risen Messiah as Lord as the agent of Gentile inclusion (section III). Three more sections address the relationship between Jesus' resurrection and the justification of the ungodly (section IV: Rom 4:17-25); Jesus' resurrection and the resurrection of believers (section V: Rom 6 – 8); and Jesus' resurrection and faith in Christ as Lord (section VI: Romans 10, 14). A series of concluding observations follow (section VII).

---

[2] For example, Fitzmyer's commentary, notable for having over 200 pages of bibliographical information, lists no monograph dedicated to the resurrection in Romans, J.A. Fitzmyer, *Romans: A New Translation with Introduction and Commentary* (AB 33; London: Geoffrey Chapman, 1993). Readers interested in tracing further reading on any of the passages or themes mentioned below will find it here.

2. Jesus' Resurrection and Paul's Apostleship (1:1–7, esp. v. 4)

In his opening salutation Paul makes a radical expansion to the core formula which might be expected for a Greco-Roman epistle: 'Paul, to the Romans, greetings.' Most obviously, he fills out his own identity in such a way as to introduce himself, specifically his gospel and his apostleship, to the Roman Christians. The progression of thought is fairly straightforward: Paul's apostolic calling involved a consecration to the gospel, a gospel which has its origin and focus in God, and which was promised in the holy Scriptures. In terms of content the gospel finds its focus in a brief poetic narrative of the career of the Son of God: his messianic ministry and his powerful resurrection to Lordship. It was this Lord Jesus Christ who is the source of Paul's apostleship, which entails bringing about the obedience of faith among all the Gentiles, thus including the recipients of the letter: the Christians at Rome.

It is widely acknowledged that in vv. 3 and 4 Paul describes the ministry of the Son of God using traditional language and terminology ('the seed of David', 'the Spirit of holiness', 'by the resurrection of the dead'), as he seeks to gain the confidence of the Roman Christians: confidence in Paul and his gospel which would enable them both to accept his appeal for unity and to support his Spanish mission. I doubt myself whether this utilization of traditional terminology provides sufficient evidence to enable the reconstruction of a pre-Pauline statement. If such terminology reassured Paul's Roman hearers that his gospel was no novelty, but stood in continuity with the faith they knew, which had been confessed since the foundational witness of Peter and the other early apostles, then that would no doubt have increased the impact of his whole argument. Nevertheless, as modern commentators are increasingly recognizing, it is the Pauline content that is crucial.

I take the parallelism of vv. 3 and 4 not as relating to the two natures of Christ in a systematic or christological sense, but as reflecting two historical modes of Christ's existence: his messianic ministry as Son of David (according to the flesh) and his subsequent enthronement as powerful Son of God (according to the Holy Spirit). A notable feature of these verses is the emphasis placed on Jesus' Davidic descent, something which although comparatively rare in the other epistles (cf. only 2 Tim. 2:8 explicitly) is prominent in Romans (cf. 9:5; 15:8f., 12) and, as we shall see, is twice connected with Jesus' resurrection and the Gentile mission. In v. 4 Paul takes the resurrection of Jesus from among the dead as the moment of his enthronement as 'Son-of-God-in-power.'

The language and thought of this verse reflects two absolutely central passages in the Old Testament, both of which played a prominent role in the eschatological expectation of first-century Judaism and in the writings of the New Testament. First, we note God's promise to David in 2 Samuel 7:12–14:

> When your days are fulfilled and you lie down with your ancestors, I will raise up your offspring after you, who shall come forth from your body, and I will establish his kingdom. He shall build a house for my name, and I will establish the throne of his kingdom forever. I will be a father to him, and he shall be a son to me.

The echoes are substantial, especially in the Greek: God will raise up the seed of David, establishing his eternal kingdom, and claiming him as his own son.

The second passage contains these same themes: the role of the Davidic king, God's pronouncement of the adoption formula and the granting of a universal kingdom. In the second psalm God announces that he will set his anointed Davidic King on Zion his holy hill:

> I will tell of the decree of the Lord: He said to me, 'You are my son; today I have begotten you.

> Ask of me, and I will make the nations your heritage, and the ends of the earth your possession.

> You shall break them with a rod of iron, and dash them in pieces like a potter's vessel' (Ps. 2:7–9).

This psalm associates the enthronement of the king with a God-given invitation to exercise a universal dominion. Paul, looking back to this psalm through the window of Jesus' resurrection (and possibly in the light of 2 Sam. 7) finds a strong connection between the resurrection of Jesus the Messiah and his messianic dominion over the nations. From this perspective the resurrection of Jesus the Messiah is both God's coronation decree, 'You are my Son', and the basis for the Messiah's universal dominion.[3]

In vv. 5 and 6 it becomes transparently clear that the risen and powerful messianic Lord has bestowed the grace of apostleship on Paul with the purpose of advancing his universal dominion over all the nations through the preaching of the gospel (the obedience of faith among all the nations). Paul's thought is thoroughly eschatological: the resurrection of Jesus is the turn of the ages and now he reigns as King.

That the resurrection marked a decisive moment in the eschatological mission of Jesus the Son is also emphasized in the speeches of Peter and Paul in Acts (Acts 2, esp. v. 36).[4] The logic of the use of the OT is closely paralleled in Paul's sermon in Pisidian Antioch (Acts 13:30–34):

> But God raised him from the dead; and for many days he appeared to those who came up with him from Galilee to Jerusalem, and they are now his witnesses to the people. And we bring you the good news that what God promised to our ancestors he has fulfilled for us, their children, by raising Jesus; as also it is written in the second psalm, 'You are my Son; today I have begotten you.' As to his raising him from the dead, no more to return to corruption, he has spoken in this way, 'I will give you the holy promises made to David.'

Here the resurrection of Jesus is associated with both Psalm 2:7, 'you are my Son; today I have begotten you', and Isaiah 55:3, 'Incline your ear, and come to me; listen, so that you may live. I will make with you an everlasting covenant, my steadfast, sure love for David.' In the sermon in Acts, Paul picks up the reference to life in the preceding phrase of the verse as, apparently, the basis for applying the second part of the verse to the risen Jesus: 'I will give you the holy promises made to David' (although we should note that the 'I will give' comes not from Isaiah 55, but from an echo of Psalm 2:8 cited earlier). The point is the same as that made in Romans 1:3f.: by virtue of his resurrection God bestows upon the messianic lord that extensive authority which was promised to the Davidic King: rulership

---

[3] See L.C. Allen, 'The Old Testament Background of (προ)ὁρίζειν in the New Testament' *New Testament Studies* 17 (1970f), 104–8.

[4] See D. Peterson's discussion in the previous chapter.

over the nations, that is, the Gentiles (cf. also Phil. 2:9–11; Mt. 28:18–20).

3. The Risen Messiah as Lord and Gentile Inclusion (15:7–13, esp. v. 12)

Anders Nygren asserted that 'in Romans 1:4 we have the whole message of the epistle in a nutshell.'[5] This suggestion is supported not only by the importance of the introductory greeting in setting the context for the reception of the epistle, but also by Paul's return to the same set of ideas in his concluding appeal to the Roman hearers. This represents a sort of *inclusio*, with the same biblical theology undergirding the start and end of Paul's argument. The key passage is 15:7–13, clearly the practical (if not theological) climax of Romans: the appeal to Jewish Christians and Gentile Christians to pull together and unite in the gospel, an appeal that the rest of Romans prepares for theologically. The theological basis for the appeal is the resurrection of Jesus as messianic King over all the nations.

'Welcome one another', says Paul (15:7) to the factions described previously as 'weak' and 'strong.' Reading between the lines of ch. 14 suggests that these factions were aligned in terms of their approach to food laws and sabbath-observance, and the welcome of Jews and Gentiles alike together becomes explicit in these following verses.[6] Christ's welcome functions as the model and the means: he welcomes freely, graciously, by faith without deeds, through his sacrificial death and powerful resurrection, and with a view to the glory of God.

In vv. 8 and 9 Paul returns to the thought of his opening verses: Christ's messianic ministry confirms the patriarchal promises: blessing to Israel and through them a blessing to all nations. Note that the gospel for the Gentiles does not in any way transcend or negate the patriarchal promises, it rather depends on Christ having fulfilled them so that the Gentiles might also 'glorify God for his saving mercy.' In the following verses Paul cites four different passages of Scripture, all of which point to

---

[5] *Commentary on Romans* (Philadelphia: Muhlenberg, 1949), 51.
[6] See especially A.J.M. Wedderburn, *The Reasons for Romans* (Edinburgh: T.& T. Clark, 1991).

the united praise of the Messiah (or the Lord) coming from Israel (his people) and the Gentiles/nations.[7] The last of these (in 15:12), the only one introduced by name, provides the rationale: 'the root of Jesse shall come, the one who rises to rule the Gentiles; in him the Gentiles shall hope' (Rom. 15:12; cf. Isa. 11:10).

The inclusion of Gentiles in the messianic people of God comes through the resurrection of the Messiah: he shall come, he shall rise, Gentiles shall hope in him.

Paul takes this passage almost directly from the LXX of Isaiah 11:10, itself already a straightforward messianic passage (cf. 11:1; also alluded to in Rev. 5:5; 22:16).[8] The terminology, using *anistēmi*, refers to resurrection in several key passages in the LXX (Isa. 26:19; Dan. 12:2; cf. Hos. 6:2; also Pss. Sol. 17.21).[9] It is also widely used of Jesus' resurrection in the rest of the NT,[10] and by Paul when he seems to be citing traditional material (as here, also 1 Thess. 4:14; cf. Acts 13:33f.; 17:3, 31; also used of believers: 1 Thess. 4:16; Eph. 5:14). While not, Paul's most customary way of referring to Jesus' resurrection, there is no doubt that this is what he refers to here.

The inclusion of the Gentiles within the saving purposes of God arises out of the resurrection of his Messiah. Jesus the messianic Lord extends his universal dominion through the preaching of the gospel and the inclusion of those from every tribe and tongue and people and nation. It remains to be seen whether these perspectives are further illuminated by an investigation of other references to Jesus' resurrection in Romans.

---

[7] Ps. 18:50 (LXX 17:50); Deut. 32:43; Ps. 118:1 (LXX 117:1); Isa. 11:10.

[8] See C.D. Stanley, *Paul and the Language of Scripture: Citation technique in the Pauline Epistles and contemporary literature* (SNTSMS 74; Cambridge: CUP, 1992), 183.

[9] Already with this sense in Greek literature from Homer, according to H.G. Liddell, R. Scott, and H.S. Jones, *A Greek-English Lexicon* (Oxford: Clarendon, 1985), 144.

[10] E.g. Mk. 8:31; 9:9f. (cf. Mt. 17:9 v.l.); 9:31; 10:34; Lk. 18:33; 24:7, 46; Jn. 20:9; Acts 2:24, 32; 10:41; cf. Mk. 16:9; Ignatius, *Rom.* 6.1; *Ep. Barn.* 15.9.

4. Jesus' Resurrection and God who justifies the ungodly (4:17–25)

After the introduction there are no references to the resurrection until several which occur in a cluster towards the end of ch. 4. Having announced God's decisive action in revealing his saving righteousness in the cross as the place where sin is dealt with (3:21ff.), Paul shows that God had always purposed to form a people of faith, following the example of Abraham: 'Abraham believed God and it was reckoned to him as righteousness.' In the later part of ch. 4 Paul outlines some important elements of the nature of Abraham's faith.

Abraham believed in God the creator (4:17), God the promiser (throughout), and God the life-giver (4:17). Abraham's faith in God contrasts with the Adamic fallenness of humanity as depicted in ch. 1 of Romans: faith in the creator, faith in his spoken promise, a faith strengthened in giving glory to God (contrast ch. 1).[11] In all of this Abraham is presented as the model of Christian faith (explicitly in 4:11f., 23ff.), not only for the Christians in Rome, but for all those who like him trust in God's gospel promise through Christ.[12] This last point is drawn out explicitly in the closing verses (4:23–5):

> Now the words, 'it was reckoned to him,' were written not for his sake alone, but for ours also. It will be reckoned to us who believe in him who raised Jesus our Lord from the dead, who was handed over to death for our trespasses and was raised for our justification.

Paul has deliberately portrayed Abraham's faith as directed towards 'God who enlivens the dead' (4:17), a traditional description in OT and Judaism which within the context is connected with his own deadness and the barrenness of Sarah's

---

[11] See further E. Adams, 'Abraham's Faith and Gentile Disobedience: Textual Links between Romans 1 and 4', *Journal for the Study of the New Testament* 65 (1997), 47–66.

[12] Paul's depiction of Abraham as 'strong' in faith matches his own description in 15:1 ('we who are strong'), and has significant echoes in ch. 14. For discussion see A. Lincoln, 'Abraham Goes to Rome: Paul's Treatment of Abraham in Romans 4' in *Worship, Theology and Ministry in the Early Church: Essays in Honor of Ralph P. Martin* (eds. M.J. Wilkins and T. Paige; JSNTSS 87; Sheffield: JSOT, 1992), 163–79.

womb (v. 19).[13] In other words, Abraham's faith in God's promise included the idea that this promise would be fulfilled through a 'resurrection.' It is possible, in view of parallels in Jewish thought, that the reference to God the creator is similarly to be oriented to his ability to bring 'resurrection.'[14] Paul's argument is clearly and deliberately constructed in order to provide a close parallel between Abraham's faith and Christian faith: faith in God who raised Jesus our Lord from the dead (a designation which quickly became a foundational Christian dogma).[15] God's gospel promises are realised through the resurrection of Jesus, although, as Paul continues, the twin axes of Jesus' saving work are his death and resurrection: 'who was handed over to death for our trespasses and was raised for our justification.'

This solemn formula brings the chapter to a close with a careful parallelism, both elements of which echo Isaiah 53 (often thought to reflect a pre-Pauline tradition).[16] Uniquely in Paul this passage connects our justification with Jesus' resurrection, and it is this connection which will be the focus of our interest here.

---

[13] Cf. Deut. 32:39; 1 Sam. 2:6; 2 Kgs. 5:7; Ps. 71:20; cf: Wisd. 16:13; Tob. 13:2; *Jos. and Asen.* 20:7; *Test. Gad* 4:6; *Shemoneh Ezreh,* etc. See R. Bauckham, 'God who raises the Dead: The Resurrection of Jesus and Early Christian Faith in God' in *The Resurrection of Jesus Christ* (ed. P. Avis; London: DLT, 1993), 136–54.

[14] In the account in 2 Macc. 7 of the eight martyrs – a mother and her seven sons – they go to their horrible deaths believing in God's power to raise them from death (see vv. 9, 11, 14, 23, 29). This resurrection power is twice associated with his power to create; cf. 2 Macc. 7.23: 'Therefore the Creator of the world, who shaped the beginning of humankind and devised the origin of all things, will in his mercy give life and breath back to you again, since you now forget yourselves for the sake of his laws' (cf. also 7:28f. for creation *ex nihilo* and resurrection hope). See O. Hofius, 'Eine altjüdische Parallele zu Röm. IV.17b', *New Testament Studies* 18 (1971f), 93–4.

[15] Cf. Acts 3:15; 4:10; 13:30; 1 Pet. 1:21; Rom. 8:11; 10:9; 1 Cor. 6:14; 15:15; 2 Cor. 4:14; Gal. 1:1; 1 Thess. 1:10; Col. 2:12; Eph. 1:20. For an interesting parallel see Josephus's version of Abraham's faith expressed in terms of Isaac's soul (*Antiquities,* 1. 231).

[16] P. Stuhlmacher, 'Jesus' Resurrection and the View of Righteousness in the Pre-Pauline Mission Congregations' in *Reconciliation, Law and Righteousness: Essays in Biblical Theology* (ET; Philadelphia: Fortress, 1986), 50–67, esp. here 55f.

The formula contains two passive verbs and two *dia* clauses. We should probably take the passives as 'divine passives': it was God who handed Jesus over (to death) for our trespasses, and it was God who raised him up for our justification. The first line echoes Isaiah 53:12, especially in the Greek version ('because of their sins he was handed over'). This suggests that the first *dia* clause may best be understood retrospectively or causally. It is difficult to understand the second *dia* in the same way as the first: how can our justification be the reason for Jesus' resurrection? Most commentators sensibly opt for a prospective or final use of *dia*: 'Christ was raised "for the sake of" / "because of the need for" our justification.'[17]

Some scholars have taken the view that the two clauses are divided only for rhetorical effect: Jesus' death and resurrection provides for forgiveness of sin and justification.[18] On the other hand, it seems likely that there may be something altogether more significant here in terms of the link between resurrection and justification. This view is made more likely when the parallel in Isaiah 53:11 is noted: the servant makes many to be accounted righteous in the context of his own vindication (possibly resurrection).[19]

But granted that Paul generally traces justification to the benefits of Jesus' death (as already in 3:24ff.; also in 5:9), what might he mean by connecting justification to Jesus' resurrection? John Murray offered five examples of 'the respects in which the resurrection of Christ may be conceived of as serving the end of justification':[20]

> Firstly, the means of justification is faith directed to Jesus, and this is only appropriately directed to Jesus the living Lord (3:22, 26).

> Secondly, justification comes about through union with Christ, a union which can only have efficacy in relation to the living Christ (8:1; 2 Cor. 5:21).

---

[17] See Moo, *Romans*, 289 n. 10 for details (cf. also Cranfield, *Romans*, vol. 1, 252).

[18] E.g. Fitzmyer, *Romans*, 389 (referring to 'many Latin fathers').

[19] So Cranfield, *Romans*, vol. 1, 252. Cf. Butterworth's essay earlier in this volume.

[20] J. Murray, *The Epistle to the Romans* (NICNT; Grand Rapids: Eerdmans, 1960), 156–7.

Thirdly, the righteousness of Christ is embodied in the risen, living Lord and thus bestowed upon believers (cf. 5:17–19; 1 Cor. 1:30).

Fourthly, the death and resurrection of Christ should be regarded as inseparable.

Fifthly, we come to stand in a justified state through the mediation of Christ, a mediation which needs his resurrection power (5:2).

It may be asked whether, notwithstanding this impressive list, there is yet more to be said in terms of a more fundamental connection between Christ's resurrection and our justification (further evidence might be gleaned from the references to salvation through Jesus' *life* in Rom. 5:10, 17f.). For Paul, the resurrection of Christ represented *his* vindication, the public declaration of his righteousness by God, in other words, his *justification* (cf. Rom. 1:3f.; 1 Cor. 15:17; esp. 1 Tim. 3:16). Christ was made sin (2 Cor. 5:21); he became a curse (Gal. 3:13); was 'in the likeness of sinful flesh' (Rom. 8:3); but this did not reflect his true standing with God, and was overturned in the resurrection. Christ took the sinful pattern of human existence, becoming what we were (sinners), so that we might become what he was and is (righteous).[21]

God 'justified' Jesus by raising him from the dead: the one verdict has already been given (following the act of obedience on the cross); by faith Christians enter into Christ and are associated with that verdict. Therefore justification for believers stems from the same act of God as does identification and participation: the resurrection of Jesus. From this perspective the resurrection of Jesus represents both the historical focal point which gives substance and definition to faith in God who enlivens the dead and the vindicatory means by which the righteous verdict of Christ can be applied to the believer.

---

[21] See further M.D. Hooker, 'Interchange and Atonement' in *From Adam to Christ: Essays on Paul* (Cambridge: CUP, 1990²), 26–41, esp. 39f. on Rom. 4.25.

5. Jesus' Resurrection and the resurrection of believers (esp. 6:4–10; 7:4; 8:11)

It would not stretch the evidence to suggest that the main point of the argument of Romans 5:12 – 8:39 is to affirm that *just as* believers have been granted that verdict of righteousness-vindication that was proclaimed in the resurrection of Jesus *so too* believers will be rescued from death and granted a part in the resurrection life of Jesus. At the point where Paul turns from the salvation-historical perspective (of 5:20f.) to the individual (seeking to return to the question first posed in 3:1–8), the unity of the believer with the Lord Jesus Christ is pivotal. This is expressed firstly in terms of the death of Jesus and the believer's death to sin (ch. 6), death of the law (ch. 7), and death to the old life (ch. 8). It is also expressed in terms of the resurrection of Jesus. In all three chapters the unity of the believer with the Lord Jesus Christ, he who died and was raised to life, involves a unity with his resurrection life. This unity has both present and future eschatological elements (something that Paul had already hinted at in passages such as 5:10).

In Rom. 6:4–10 Paul raises a number of important issues. The basic structure of the argument concerns the believer's deadness to sin, based on the identification of the believer with Christ's death:

> Do you not know that all of us who have been baptized into Christ Jesus were baptized into his death? Therefore we have been buried with him by baptism into death . . . (Rom 6:3–4a).[22]

Associated with this is the resurrection-tension which runs through this section: while believers have been united with Christ in a death like his (a decisive death in relation to sin), their association with Christ's resurrection seems to have a twofold aspect: present transformation ('the newness of life', 6:4, 11); and future complete transformation (6:5, 8).

Without entering into a detailed discussion of this passage, it is clear that the eschatological perspective of Paul here is

---

[22] We should note in passing that the burial of Jesus is an important aspect of Paul's thought (Rom. 6:3; 1 Cor. 15:4; Col. 2:12). This, in combination with Paul's belief in the physical resurrection (as attested throughout 1 Cor. 15), coheres fully with the empty-tomb tradition (cf. Acts 13:29).

fundamentally that which he also expressed in 1 Corinthians 15. Christ was raised as the first-fruits and the resurrection and associated transformation of believers, while assured, remains a future expectation associated with Christ's completed victory over death. This is asserted in Rom. 6:6f. In Adam we all share in a solidarity of sin and death (as Paul has explained in Rom. 5:12–21); this solidarity has been broken by Christ's death: we are included into Christ, identified with him.

The logic of ch. 6 as a whole – that unity with Christ in his death and resurrection enables a new aliveness to God – is echoed in compact form, in relation to the Torah, in 7:4. Immediately prior to this, Paul has stated his general principle in v.1 – the Law is binding only during life – and illustrated this principle from the practice that the marriage bond is anulled by the death of a partner (vv. 2 and 3). He then makes two points of application in v. 4: (a) a death frees one from the law; and (b) such a death makes a new relationship possible – the believer freed from the law is bound to the one who died and rose again.

The elucidation of this statement in vv. 5 and 6 involves both a strong temporal contrast ('we were then . . . but now . . .') and the introduction of a reference to the Holy Spirit (v. 6): the new life (already mentioned in ch. 6 as the consequence of resurrection with Christ) is here ascribed to the Spirit:

> While we were living in the flesh, our sinful passions, aroused by the law, were at work in our members to bear fruit for death. But now we are discharged from the law, dead to that which held us captive, so that we are slaves not under the old written code but in the new life of the Spirit.

How is this resurrection life, promised both in the present and in the eschatological future, realized in the life of the believer? The answer, specified especially in Rom. 8:10f., is clear: 'through the work of the Holy Spirit':

> if Christ is in you (through the indwelling Spirit living in every believer), then while the body is dead because of sin, the spirit is life because of righteousness. If the Spirit of he who raised Jesus from the dead dwells in you, he who raised Christ from the dead will give life to even your mortal bodies, through his indwelling Spirit in you. (Rom. 8:10f.)

These verses are somewhat difficult, due in part to the compact nature of Paul's expression, but it seems likely that Paul is affirming the Holy Spirit's role in the enlivening of our dead sinful bodies in this life (v. 10) and in the resurrection of our dead physical bodies in a future existence (v. 11). We shall have to defend this understanding briefly.

In 8:10b 'the body dead because of sin' seems to refer to the physical body of the believer in its subjection to death because of sin (hence the solution in the next verse is resurrection). The following phrase, 'the spirit is life because of righteousness', most probably refers to the enlivening activity of the Holy Spirit.[23] The present provision for the deadness of the body is thus the life-bringing activity of the indwelling Spirit.

In v. 11 Paul continues the argument with a new focus on the final resurrection of the believer indwelt by the Spirit. God the Father is twice described as the one who raised Jesus/Christ from the dead (cf. Rom. 4:24).[24] The indwelling Spirit functions as both the guarantee and the agent of final resurrection. The God who gives life will enliven the bodies subject to death through the indwelling Spirit.[25] The fact that the *agency* of the

---

[23] It is true the *pneuma* might refer (as in v. 16) to the human spirit, as alive through the righteousness of Christ (with NIV, RSV). But in these verses *pneuma* occurs with reference to the Holy Spirit 11 times in as many verses, and when Paul does refer to the human spirit (in v. 16) he does so unambiguously with an appropriate pronoun (the Spirit bears witness with our spirit). This, Calvin's view, has become more popular in recent years (note esp. NRSV, Dunn, Cranfield, Fee).

[24] It is notable that Paul first refers to God as 'the one who raised Jesus from the dead' and subsequently as 'the one who raised Christ from the dead'. No doubt the point of the double reference to the resurrection of Jesus is that Paul is building upon the close connection which exists between the resurrection of Jesus Christ and the resurrection of believers (as he has expounded at great length in 1 Cor. 15; cf. also 1 Cor. 6:14; 2 Cor. 4:14; Phil. 3:21; 1 Thess. 4:14). If we are entitled to note the change from 'Jesus' to 'Christ' we might suggest that Paul moves from the historical event of the resurrection (using Jesus) to the importance of that for all those who relate to Jesus as Messiah (with Cranfield). This is even more powerful if we recall our conclusion from an earlier section: that it is precisely in his role as risen Messiah that the Lord Jesus exercises his saving sovereignty over all nations.

[25] The language used here, specifically *zōopoieō* ('to make alive', 'give life to'), is customarily used of resurrection, often synonymous with *egeirō* (e.g. Jn. 5:21; 1 Cor. 15:22 (cf. 36, 45); 1 Pet. 3:18; 2 Kgs. 5:7 (LXX)). Hence the almost universal opinion among commentators that what is spoken of here is the final resurrection of the dead bodies of believers. The alternative view, that it might be used of an enlivening experienced in this life (so Calvin; and cf. 4:17), is

Spirit in the future resurrection is nowhere else specified in the NT, and a large number of early manuscripts read here a *dia* followed by an accusative (i.e. 'because of his indwelling Spirit'), has led some scholars to deny that this is what Paul is asserting here; rather the emphasis is purely on the assurance of future resurrection.[26] Nevertheless, the textual evidence is divided, with most editions and translations reading *dia* followed by a gentive (i.e. 'through/by means of his indwelling Spirit'); the agency of the Holy Spirit in connection with Jesus' resurrection is apparently supported by Paul (cf. Rom. 1:4; 1 Tim. 3:16; 1 Cor. 6:14); and the agency of the Holy Spirit in connection with the future resurrection of believers, which seems to be assumed by the argument here, is apparently everywhere assumed in Jewish thought reflecting on Ezekiel 37:14.[27]

6. Jesus' Resurrection and faith in Christ as Lord (esp. 10:7–9; 14:9–11)

The next references to Jesus' resurrection in Romans come in the midst of ch. 10 in a description of a believing response to the basic content of Paul's gospel preaching:

> because if you confess with your lips that Jesus is Lord and believe in your heart that God raised him from the dead, you will be saved. For one believes with the heart and so is justified, and one confesses with the mouth and so is saved. For the Scripture says, 'Everyone who believes in him will not be put to shame' (Rom. 10:9–11).

We do well to take note of this final verse (v. 11 citing Isa. 28:16), rather than simply citing vv. 9 and 10, because it alerts us both

---

rejected by Cranfield because the final resurrection view, he argues, fits better with v. 10, the use of 'mortal', the language of v. 13 and the fact that v. 12 seems to start a new section.

[26] E.g. G.D. Fee, *God's Empowering Presence: The Holy Spirit in the Letters of Paul* (Peabody, MA: Hendrickson, 1994), 553.

[27] Ezek. 37:14a: 'I will put my spirit within you, and you shall live'; cf. 2 Bar. 21:4; 23:5; *4 Ezra* 6.39–41; *m. Sota* 9.15; *Genesis Rabbah* 14.8; 96.5; *Exodus Rabbah* 48.4; *Canticles Rabbah* 1.1 #9; *Midrash Psalms* 85.3; *Pesiqta Rabbati* 1.6; cf. also 2 Macc. 7.22; *Jos. and Asen.* 8.9; 2nd of 18 Benedictions (from M.M.B. Turner, *The Holy Spirit and Spiritual Gifts: Then and Now* (Carlisle: Paternoster, 1996), 125).

to the destination of Paul's argument and its point of departure. The destination is the universal availability of salvation (vv. 12 and 13), to which we shall return in a moment. The point of departure is the earlier and fuller citation of this same passage in 9:33: 'See, I am laying in Zion a stone that will make people stumble, a rock that will make them fall, and whoever believes in him will not be put to shame.' Paul has been contrasting the righteousness based on faith (which Gentiles have received), with the righteousness based on Torah, which Israel strived for but did not attain. Israel failed to gain God's saving-righteousness because they failed to acknowledge Christ, the one to whom the Law all along was leading.[28] Christ, says Paul in one of his more enigmatic assertions, is the goal of the Torah (that to whom Torah always pointed and in whom the era of Torah is brought to an end) so that there may be a righteousness for everyone who believes (9:30 – 10:4).

The next section (vv. 5–13) is basically an explanation of the second part of v. 4. It opens with an expression of the righteousness based on Torah: it requires doing (Lev. 18:5), but turns more fully into an expression of the righteousness based on faith (based on Deut. 30:11–14). This faith-righteousness, like the covenant promise of Deuteronomy, does not cry out for human effort to gain God's favour, vv. 6f.:

> the righteousness that comes from faith says, 'Do not say in your heart, "Who will ascend into heaven?"' (that is to bring Christ down); 'or "Who will descend into the abyss?"' (that is to bring Christ up from the dead).

Rather, this faith-righteousness says: 'The word is near you, on your lips and in your heart.' It is this nearness of the word (perhaps with the added thought that its nearness comes from Christ's incarnation and resurrection) that Paul claims in identifying his gospel preaching with the covenant word: that word of which the Scripture speaks is the word of faith which we are preaching.

---

[28] The further failure of Israel, which is the larger context of our passage, is highlighted by their rejection, despite ample opportunity (v. 14–17), of the gospel message (cf. vv. 18–21).

Verses 9 and 10 then pick up the two locations, mouth and heart, and explain the metaphor of nearness in terms of confession and faith in Christ the risen Lord. God's saving righteousness is granted to all those who believe in the one who, having been a stumbling stone laid in Zion, was raised from the dead to become Lord of all. The unusual order involved in referring to confession before he refers to faith (unusual because confession arises from faith), is required by the OT saying previously cited and is in fact reversed in v. 10 and again in the following section in terms of faith (v. 11) and the invocation of the name of the Lord (v. 13). This, in addition to the general use of 'salvation' terminology (vv. 9, 10, 13), as well as the similarity of content, suggests the propriety of taking the two elements together. As Cranfield said: 'the two formulations interpret each other, so that what is to be both believed and confessed is the more precisely defined.'[29]

The affirmation of Jesus as Lord, so characteristic of early Christianity,[30] arose from the resurrection, hence the combination here in these verses. No doubt the application to Christ of Joel 2:32 (cf. Acts 2), which speaks originally about Yahweh the Lord, is of immense christological significance (cf. 1 Cor. 2:16; Phil. 2:11; 1 Thess. 5:2; 2 Thess. 2:2).[31] The underlying theology we have discerned previously, both in Romans 1 and in ch. 4, is that by his resurrection Jesus is granted that universal lordship which is appropriate to the Messiah, and as universal Lord he bestows his grace to all those who call upon him, both Jews and Gentiles. In the new era inaugurated by his resurrection, gospel proclamation displaces the commandments just as Christ displaces the law as the locus (or focus) of God's dealings with his people. And all those who confess and believe enter the new community, based on saving-righteousness of God, devoted to the same Lord.

---

[29] Cranfield, *Romans*, vol. 2, 527. The different view is defended in W. Sanday and A.C. Headlam, *A Critical and Exegetical Commentary on the Epistle to the Romans* (ICC; Edinburgh: T.&T. Clark, 1895), 290.

[30] Evidence for this is found primarily in the Aramaic formula preserved in 1 Cor. 16:22 (cf. Rev. 22:20; *Didache* 10.6); for additional evidence see Acts 2:36; Phil. 2:11//Ps. 110:1; 1 Cor. 8:5f//Deut 6:4).

[31] See Cranfield, *Romans*, vol. 2, 529; further D.B. Capes, *Old Testament Yahweh Texts in Paul's Christology* (WUNT II.47, Tübingen: J.C.B. Mohr, 1992).

It is precisely this which also explains why an appeal to the resurrection of Jesus is central to Paul's advice to the weak and the strong (14:9–11): Christ's death and resurrection have established him as Lord of all his people, this means that our actions are done first and foremost in relation to Christ the Lord who will judge justly, and not for the benefit of others, who may judge or condemn inappropriately.[32]

7. Conclusion

We have covered a good deal of ground and even so have only begun to scratch the surface of this incredible document. Without meaning to sideline any of the many observations made throughout this paper it should be possible, in conclusion, to highlight three areas of importance for our understanding of Pauline theology and then make two final observations.

First and foremost, this discussion has highlighted the importance and attention that must be given to the OT background of Paul's thought if we are to make sense of his teaching on the resurrection, especially in relation to the eschatological orientation of his thought. Now that Messiah is raised he exercises his universal lordly domain by calling Gentiles to himself through the proclamation of the gospel without forcing them to come by way of the Torah. In *our* preaching and evangelism we continue to do the same.

Second, I think it is possible to conclude that the centrality of the resurrection for Paul and its role as a shared assumption in his presentation in Romans (as suggested by the traditional nature of much of Paul's resurrection language) supports the conclusion that belief in the resurrection of Jesus was the shared

---

[32] This would be even clearer if Paul understood the 'as I live' of 14:11 as referring to the resurrection of Jesus the Lord. For *zaō* used of resurrection see 14:9 (note the emphasis here on Christ's universal lordship which is picked up from Isa. 45:23); Rom. 6:11; 2 Cor. 13:4 ('for he was crucified in weakness, but lives by the power of God') (cf. analogously 2 Cor. 4:11; Gal. 2:19f.; 1 Thess. 5:10); elsewhere in the NT (re Jesus): Lk. 24:5, 23; Acts 1:3; Rev. 1:18; 2:8 (cf. Mk. 16:11). See further M. Black, 'The Christological Use of the Old Testament in the New Testament', *New Testament Studies* 18 (1971f), 1–14, esp. 8; L.J. Kreitzer, *Jesus and God in Paul's Eschatology* (JSNTSS 19; Sheffield: Sheffield Academic, 1987), 107–12.

and universal faith of the earliest Christian communities. In my opinion the best historical explanation for this shared conviction remains the Bible's assertion that it actually happened in Jerusalem in the early AD 30s.

Third, although much of this is clearly of universal significance, it was also of specific and strategic importance in persuading the mixed churches of Rome to support Paul's gospel mission to Spain. The resurrection of Jesus is the primary basis in Romans for the unity of Jew and Gentile believers. My two concluding observations draw upon reflecting on the possible impact of this letter.

One of the features of Paul's thought is that Christian faith and confession is focused on the resurrection-lordship of Jesus. Christians confess the public truth that 'Jesus is Lord', and understand that lordship to have been conferred at and by his resurrection (Rom. 1:4; 4:24; 10:9f.; 14:9). Thus consistency of faith and confession is absolutely necessary, as Paul affirms, 'if you confess with your lips that Jesus is Lord and believe in your heart that God raised him from the dead, you will be saved' (Rom. 10:9). Partly because of the success and confidence of Christian testimony to Christ's Lordship in Rome, and also because of the increasingly arrogant utilization of divine titles by emperors (from Nero onwards), Christians in Rome could easily come into conflict with the claim that the emperor was 'Lord.' Indeed, less than a decade after the writing of this epistle, Nero had countless Christians put to death in the city of Rome because of their confession (presumably that Jesus was Lord). The scene after the fire of Rome is recorded in a well-known passage in Tacitus:

> Therefore, to abolish the rumour [that Nero himself was responsible for the fire] Nero substituted culprits and inflicted most extreme punishments on those, hateful by reason of their abominations, who were commonly called Christians. Christus, the originator of that name, had been executed by the procurator Pontius Pilate. The pernicious superstition, checked for the moment, was bursting out again not only throughout Judaea, the birthplace of the plague, but also throughout the city into which all that is horrible and shameful streams from every quarter and is constantly practised. Therefore, first *those who confessed* were arrested, then on their information a huge throng was convicted not so much on a charge of arson as because of their hatred of the

human race. Mockery was added as they perished, so that they died wither covered by the skins of wild beasts and torn to pieces by hounds or were nailed on crosses to be set on fire and when daylight failed were burnt to give illumination by night. Nero had offered his own gardens for the spectacle and produced a show like that of the games, mingling with the common people in the dress of a charioteer or driving his chariot (Tacitus, *Annals* 15.44).

This is a sobering account. Many of those who heard this letter read in their gatherings were called upon to maintain their confession even unto death. This ought to remind us that to confess faith in Jesus the risen Lord is to commit ourselves to living and dying in submission to his will. Ironically Tacitus himself helps us to see in their deaths a beacon of light lighting up the darkness. For them, as for us, the sure and certain hope of the resurrection from the dead provided assurance. This introduces my second concluding observation.

In the Jewish catacombs of Monteverde, the oldest of all the Jewish catacombs in Rome,[33] reflecting Jewish thought in the Western diaspora, there are a large number of epitaphs, or funerary inscriptions. Among these inscriptions 'there is precious little evidence of hope in an afterlife, and even less of the resurrection' reflecting, more than likely 'a syncretistic assimiltation to the religious-cultural conceptions of the milieu.'[34] One rather pessimistic formula, which recurs on at least five inscriptions, is simply: 'Be brave, no one is immortal.'[35] Into this context the confident Christian assertion that God had broken into human history in the resurrection of Messiah Jesus doubtless offered both new hope and new life in the gospel to many. Indeed the later Christian catacombs reflect a much stronger eschatological confidence with numerous

---

[33] This is considered to be the oldest of the catacombs because of its lack of pictures and cubicles, because only here are there inscriptions in Hebrew, and because of the presence of bricks with a first-century date stamp. See R. Penna, 'The Jews in Rome at the Time of the Apostle Paul' in *Paul The Apostle: Jew and Greek Alike* (Minnesota: Liturgical, 1996), vol. 1 26–7 (with refs.).

[34] Penna, 'The Jews in Rome at the Time of the Apostle Paul', 44 (both quotations). Cf. further H.C.C. Cavallin, *Life After Death. Paul's Argument for the Resurrection of the Dead in 1 Cor. 15. Part I: An Enquiry into the Jewish Background* (Lund: Gleerup, 1974).

[35] Penna, 'The Jews in Rome at the Time of the Apostle Paul', 42 (with refs.).

portraits reflecting confidence in resurrection to life.[36] We cannot, of course, trace this specifically to the influence of Paul's letter to the Romans, but the change in outlook is notable. Surely our 'hopeless' contemporaries need to see lives dominated by resurrection-faith and hear the message of the resurrection so that men and women can find hope and life in Christ.

Questions for further study

1. How does Paul's approach to Jesus' resurrection in Romans compare with that of Luke–Acts?

2. How persuasive is the analysis of Romans 4:25 presented in this chapter?

3. Are there important emphases in other letters of Paul not mentioned in this study of Romans?

4. To what extent is Paul's theology dominated by his vision of God?

5. How might this understanding of Paul's theology be applied to your Christian life and your church's mission?

6. Is it legitimate to use information deduced from Romans to support the historicity of Jesus' resurrection?

Select Bibliography

Bauckham, R., 'God who raises the Dead: The Resurrection of Jesus and Early Christian Faith in God' in *The Resurrection of Jesus Christ* (ed. P. Avis; London: DLT, 1993), 136–54

Clark, T.R., *Saved by His Life: A Study of the New Testament Doctrine of Reconciliation and Salvation* (New York: Macmillan, 1959)

Stanley, D.M., *Christ's Resurrection in Pauline Soteriology* (Analecta Biblica 13; Rome: Pontifical Biblical Institute, 1976[2])

---

[36] See J. Stevenson, *The Catacombs: Rediscovered monuments of early Christianity* (London: Thames & Hudson, 1978).

Wedderburn, A.J.M., *Baptism and Resurrection: Studies in Pauline Theology against Its Graeco-Roman Background* (WUNT 44; Tübingen: J.C.B. Mohr, 1987)

Four

The Resurrection of Jesus in English Puritan Thought

RUDI HEINZE

1. Introduction

In his recent study of American Puritanism, Allen Carden commented on 'the relative scarcity in Puritan preaching of references to the resurrection of Christ, a central doctrine of the faith.' He pointed out that the atoning death of Christ was the central emphasis in Puritan theology and the resurrection was simply 'expected as a "natural" ending to his earthly ministry.'[1] Although this is the only comment on the resurrection in his entire book, Carden at least mentioned what he considered to be the Puritan view of the resurrection, unlike other writers. Despite the great interest in Puritanism in the last two decades which has resulted in a flood of books dealing with Puritan teaching on almost every conceivable subject, most secondary

---

[1] A. Carden, *Puritan Christianity in America* (Grand Rapids: Baker, 1990), 75.

works do not comment on the role of the resurrection in Puritan thought.[2]

For example, James Packer in his excellent recent study of Puritan Christianity does not comment on the Puritan view of the resurrection even though he devotes an entire section to 'Puritans and the Gospel.' In his discussion of Puritan preaching he maintains that the central theme was the crucifixion 'for this is the hub of the Bible. The preacher's commission is to declare the whole counsel of God, but the cross is the centre of that counsel.' Packer's list of Puritan sermon topics fails to mention the resurrection as a specific topic, despite including 'God, sin, the cross, Christ's heavenly ministry, the Holy Spirit, faith and hypocrisy, assurance and the lack of it, prayer, meditation, temptation, mortification, growth in grace, death, heaven.'[3] Gavin McGrath also did not deal with the resurrection in his valuable published lecture on John Owen's theology of the cross. The resurrection was mentioned twice, but only as a passing comment.[4]

On initial analysis it may seem that these writers are correct in implying that Puritans did not place a great emphasis on the resurrection in their preaching or their theology. For example, the Westminster Confession gives relatively little attention to the resurrection. Although a full chapter is devoted to God's 'Eternal Decree' and a second to 'Effectual Calling', the resurrection is mentioned only briefly in four chapters. The only extended discussion is found in the Larger Catechism.[5]

---

[2] Good bibliographies of recent works are found in C. Durston and J. Eales (eds.), *The Culture of English Puritanism 1560–1700* (London: Macmillan, 1996); M. Todd, *Christian Humanism and the Puritan Social Order* (Cambridge: CUP, 1987); L. Ryken, *Worldly Saints* (Grand Rapids: Zondervan, 1986); D Wallace, *Puritans and Predestination* (Chapel Hill: University of North Carolina, 1982). A recent work which does give substantial attention to the role of the resurrection is P. Blackham, 'The Pneumatology of Thomas Goodwin' (PhD Dissertation University of London, 1995).

[3] J.I. Packer, *Among God's Giants: Aspects of Puritan Christianity* (Eastbourne: Kingsway, 1991), 376.

[4] G. McGrath, *'But We Preach Christ Crucified': The Cross of Christ in the Pastoral Theology of John Owen 1616–1683* (St Antolin's Lectureship Charity Lecture, 1994), 12 and 21.

[5] *Westminster Confession of Faith* (Glasgow: Free Presbyterian, 1985). Chapters 3 and 10; 8.4, 11.4, 12.1 and 26.1 mention the resurrection of Christ. Question 52 in the Larger Catechism states that Christ rose 'by his own power

In addition, a number of recent writers have emphasized the fear and insecurity that resulted from Puritan theology which would seem to be in direct contrast to a theology which placed a great emphasis on the resurrection. In his recent study of Nehemiah Wallington, a London Puritan artisan, Paul Seaver stressed the suicidal despair which Wallington experienced as he diligently examined his life for signs of his election and struggled against sin and temptation.[6] In a review article Blair Worden commented: 'Our temptation is to soften the Puritan mentality and, as we suppose to humanise it . . . yet we err if we neglect the darkness of Puritanism at least in its 17th century form. The volume of despair engendered by Puritan teaching on predestination is incalculable.'[7]

This argument has been developed in John Stachniewski's book entitled *The Persecutory Imagination: English Puritanism and the Literature of Religious Despair*.[8] Stachniewski reacts against the tendency to emphasize what he calls 'the brighter side' of Puritanism. In contrast he stresses the way in which the doctrine of double predestination led to despair and even suicide. The problem of determining whether one had been elected or rejected by God created a culture of introspection in which Puritans anxiously examined every detail of their daily life for signs of God's favour or displeasure. Since the reprobate might have temporary faith and exhibit all the characteristics of the elect the problem was how to distinguish temporary faith from the faith of the elect. The doubt and fear resulting from this

---

whereby he declared himself to be the Son of God, to have satisfied divine justice, to have vanquished death, and him that had the power of it, and to be Lord of quick and dead: all which he did as a public person, the head of his church, for their justification, quickening in grace, support against enemies, and to assure them of their resurrection from the dead at the last day' 153–4.

[6] 'If Wallington was in any way typical of that troubled generation, uncertainty, examination and the constant need of renewal must have characterised their whole lives. Life was a pilgrimage from which there could necessarily be no rest short of the grave.' P. Seaver, *Wallington's World: A Puritan Artisan in Seventeenth-Century London* (Stanford: Stanford University Press, 1985), 196.

[7] B. Worden, 'Calvinisms: Review of Paul S. Seaver, *Wallington's World: A Puritan Artisan in Seventeenth-Century London*', *London Review of Books* (23 Jan. to 6 Feb. 1986), 16–17.

[8] Oxford: Clarendon, 1991.

dilemma sometimes created a suicidal despair in many earnest people who became trapped by the process of introspection.

Stachniewski offers a good deal of evidence to illustrate the despair which many Puritans felt and which they expressed in their autobiographies, but, as at least one reviewer has pointed out, his presentation is very one-sided as he fails to recognize the more positive aspects of Puritan theology: 'There is joy, too, music and dancing in the Father's house. And in the preachers and guides to godliness as a whole, hard and fearsome passages apart, there are some remarkable affirmations of the Divine love, in the great tradition of Augustine, Anselm and Bernard of Clairvaux.'[9]

Those affirmations are certainly found in Puritan comments on the resurrection. Contrary to the impression given by the lack of comment in secondary works, Puritans clearly considered the resurrection one of the central doctrines of the Christian faith. The comfort, joy and reassurance which Christians should find in the resurrection of Jesus Christ was a recurring theme in Puritan sermons and treatises. Puritans wrote a great deal about the resurrection and at least for some English Puritans it was a common sermon topic. Even writers like John Owen, who tended to emphasize the cross and death of Christ more than the resurrection, called the resurrection 'the completing act in laying the foundation of the church . . . the great testimony given unto the finishing of the work of redemption.'[10] They can also

---

[9] G. Wakefield, 'Review of *The Persecutory Imagination: English Puritans and the Literature of Religious Despair* by John Stachniewski', *Journal of Theological Studies* 43 (1997), 753.

[10] J. Owen, *The Works of John Owen*, ed. by W.H. Gould (Edinburgh: T. & T. Clark, 1862), vol. 3, 179. The index to these *Works* lists only 4 references to the resurrection compared to 27 to the cross and the death of Christ. Although Owen wrote an entire book on the death of Christ, the resurrection is mentioned only when commenting on Romans 4:25 and 1 Corinthians 15:22 in order to argue that these passages do not teach universal atonement (vol. 10, 182, 352).

His most extended discussions of the resurrection were in response to the *Twofold Catechism* of the Unitarian John Biddle and in his treatise on the work of the Holy Spirit. In his *Catechism* Biddle had used Bible passages to establish that God raised Christ from the dead rather than Christ raising himself (*A Twofold Catechism* (London, J. Cottrel 1654), 77). In his response Owen pointed out that Biddle began with the assumption that Christ was not God, and went on to argue 'it is true that Christ is said to be raised by God taken

never be accused of dealing with a subject in a superficial way. The nineteenth century editor of Stephen Charnock's works was not exaggerating when he wrote: 'It may be allowed that Puritan preachers . . . carried their subdivisions too far. They sought by abstraction to bring into distinct view all the attributes of the concrete subject, and by mental analysis to distribute a complex subject into its parts. As correct thinkers their judgement would have been offended if a single one of the parts which go to make up the whole had been left out.'[11]

This incredible thoroughness was characteristic of Puritan comments on the resurrection; consequently, it is necessary to limit this study to English Puritans and to concentrate on a few writers who provide a representative sample of the Puritan tradition. Four English Puritans have been selected for special consideration: William Perkins (1588–1602), Thomas Goodwin (1600–80), Stephen Charnock (1628–80), and Thomas Manton (1620–77), because the resurrection was a common subject in their writings and sermons. They also represent a number of different Puritan traditions, and their works cover a period stretching from Elizabeth's reign (1558–1603) to the reign of Charles II (1660–85).

2. William Perkins (1558–1602)

One could hardly write about Puritan theology without beginning with William Perkins. Perkins was a Fellow of Christ's College, Cambridge, until 1595 when he became Lecturer at St. Andrews' the Great, in the same city, until his death in 1602. A noted preacher and prolific writer he influenced many undergraduates who later became Puritan leaders. Ian Breward, the modern editor of his works, calls him 'the most widely known theologian of the Elizabethan Church.' Breward points out that 'by the end of the sixteenth century he had replaced

---

personally for the Father, whose joint power with his own, and that also of the Spirit, was put forth in this work of raising Christ from the death' (*Works*, vol. 12, 561). In his treatise on the work of the Holy Spirit Owen discussed the role of the Holy Spirit in the Resurrection (*Works*, vol. 4, 181–3).

[11] J. McCosh, 'Introduction', *The Complete Works of Stephen Charnock* (Edinburgh: James Nichol, 1866), vol. 1, xxxiii.

Calvin and Beza near the top of the English religious best-seller list.'[12] Packer maintains that Perkins 'more than anyone . . . crystallised and delimited the essence of mainstream Puritan Christianity . . . imparting to it qualities that were to characterise it for the next hundred years.'[13] He was a moderate Puritan who worked well within the structures of the Church of England, readily accepting its church polity and, on the whole, conforming to the Prayer Book. He wrote extensively on the resurrection and in this area, as in many others, he had a clear influence on those who followed.

It is important at the outset to stress that Perkins viewed the resurrection as more than an intellectual concept; it was something which must be experienced by the believer. In his *A Declaration of the True Manner of Knowing Christ*, published in 1596, he first mentioned the resurrection in the context of a discussion of the crucifixion. After stating that the same power whereby Christ raised himself from death 'serveth to raise those that belong to Christ, from their sins in this life, and from the grave in the day of the last judgement', he stated that this knowledge

> must not be only speculative, that is, barely conceived in the brain, but it must be experimental: because we ought to have experience of it in our hearts and lives, and we should labour by all means possible, to feel the power of Christ's death, killing and mortifying our sins and the virtue of his resurrection, in the putting of spiritual life into us that we may be able to say, that we live not but that Christ lives in us.[14]

A more extended discussion of the resurrection is found later in the same work. In typical fashion Perkins organized his material into a series of categories which included five questions about the resurrection, eight effects of the resurrection and two uses of the doctrine concerning the resurrection. He also divided some of those categories into a number of subdivisions. Even that

[12] I. Breward, *The Work of William Perkins* (Abingdon: Sutton Courtenay, 1970), xi.
[13] J.I. Packer, *An Anglican to remember: William Perkins Puritan Popularizer* (St Antholin Lecture, 1996), 1–2.
[14] W. Perkins, *The Works of That Famous and Worthy Minister of Christ in the University of Cambridge Mr. William Perkins* (3 vols; London: John Haviland, 1631), vol. 1, 628.

discussion was not as complete as his comments on the resurrection in an earlier work entitled *An Exposition of the Symbol or Creed of the Apostles*, first published in 1595. It is therefore probably best to begin with that work and include material from his other works when they add to our understanding of Perkins' doctrine.

In this 1595 exposition of the Creed, Perkins divided his discussion into five categories: (1) why Christ rose, (2) how he rose, (3) when he rose, (4) proofs of the resurrection, and (5) the uses of the doctrine. Although it is not possible in a short paper to provide a detailed study, a brief consideration of each point is a useful way to outline the way in which Perkins explained and utilized the doctrine of the resurrection. The emphasis throughout Perkins' discussion is pastoral. This is illustrated in each of the categories listed above.

In response to the question 'Why?', Perkins stated that Christ rose to show that he had overcome death. Furthermore, since he was the Son of God and 'therefore the author of life itself',[15] it was not possible for him to remain dead. He also rose to apply the satisfaction for sin won on the cross to every believer. On the cross he made satisfaction for sin and by the resurrection the 'virtue of this sacrifice' was applied to every believer. In the resurrection he declared himself to have made a full and perfect satisfaction for sin; thus our justification was completed by the resurrection. In *The True Manner of Knowing Christ* Perkins stated this very specifically, pointing out in his discussion of the effects of the resurrection that 'the fourth effect is justification.' Even Old Testament believers were justified through the resurrection:

> When he was upon the cross, he stood there in our room having our sins imputed unto him: and when he rose from death, he acquitted and justified himself from our sins, and ceased to be any more a reputed sinner for us, and thus all that do or shall believe in him, are acquitted, absolved and justified from all their sins. If any demand, how they which lived in the time of the Old Testament, before the resurrection of Christ, could be justified thereby, considering the effect must follow the cause: I answer that they were justified by the future resurrection of Christ which

---

[15] Ibid. 235.

though it followed in time, yet did the value and virtue thereof reach even to the beginning of the world.[16]

Perkins divided his discussion of 'how' Jesus rose into five points. The first two points were central to his theology of the resurrection and need more extended comment than the final three. First, he pointed out that Jesus rose 'as a public person', representing all believers. He rose in our stead and therefore 'the whole church rose in him, and together with him.'[17] This should be a great source of comfort to the believer. In fact, in his 1596 treatise he called it 'the ground of our comfort.'[18]

Second, Christ raised himself by his own power. The fact that Christ raised himself proved that he is not only man but 'also true God' since the human body was dead and therefore 'could not bring soul and body together again and restore body to life . . . therefore there was some other nature in Christ, namely his Godhead, which did reunite soul and body together and thereby quicken the manhood.' Perkins viewed this as a great source of comfort to the believer, because, if Christ raised himself, how much more is he able to raise up 'his members from death to life.'[19] The last three points under this category were that Christ rose with an earthquake, showing that he had lost none of his power through death, that angels ministered to him and that he did not rise alone, 'but accompanied with others.'[20]

Perkins devoted a good deal less space to the third question concerning when Christ rose. He answered it by simply stating that Christ rose on the morning of the day after the Sabbath, having spent a full day and parts of two other days in the grave. However, even this seemingly obvious factual statement was used to speak a word of comfort. Perkins pointed out that since Christ arose when he was in captivity and bondage to death it establishes that 'the resurrection is a full victory and conquest over death and all our spiritual enemies.'[21]

Perkins' discussion of the proofs of the resurrection was the lengthiest part of his discussion and once again he used it as a

[16] Ibid. 664.
[17] Ibid. 235.
[18] Ibid. 663.
[19] Ibid. 235.
[20] Ibid. 236.
[21] Ibid. 663.

source of comfort for the sinner who might feel overwhelmed by
sin and failures on the road to sanctification. He based his proofs
on Jesus' appearances and the testimonies of those who
witnessed the resurrection. In commenting on Jesus'
appearance to Mary Magdalene, he maintained that the fact that
Jesus appeared first to a person who had been possessed of
seven devils reveals 'Christ is ready and willing to receive the
most miserable wretched sinners, even such as have been vessels
and bound slaves of the devil.'[22]

Further, the fact that Jesus told the women to tell the disciples
about the resurrection even though they had abandoned him in
his time of suffering, teaches 'that howsoever our sins past are to
humble us in regard of ourselves, yet must they not cut off, or
dismay us from seeking Christ, yea even then when we are laded
with the burden of them, we must come unto him, and he will
ease us.'[23] Even the disciples, who were taught by Christ 'and
often catechised in this very point of Christ's resurrection', did
not initially believe.[24] This refutes those who say that it is easy to
believe in Christ and who insist they never experience doubt.
Although he did not say so specifically, the implication was that
this should be a source of comfort to those whose faith is weak.
This is specifically taught in Christ's dealing with Thomas as he
showed his mercy and compassion even to one who had great
doubt and whose faith seemed to have been lost:

> He might have rejected Thomas for his wilfulness, yet to help his
> unbelief, he yielded unto his weakness. This sheweth that Christ is
> most compassionate to all those that unfailedly repent them of
> their sins and cleave unto him, although they do it laden with
> manifold wants . . . When a child is very sick, in so much that it
> casteth up all the meat that it taketh, the mother will not be
> offended thereat, but rather pity it. Now our Saviour Christ is ten
> thousand times more merciful to them that believe in him, than
> any mother is or can be . . . And in this example of Thomas we
> may see the estate of God's people in this life. First, God giveth the
> faith, yet afterward for a time he doth (as it were) hide the same
> in some corner of their hearts, so as they have no feeling thereof,
> but think themselves to be void of all grace and this he doth for no

---

22 Ibid. 237.
23 Ibid. 238.
24 Ibid.

other end but to humble them and yet again after all this the first
grace is further renewed and revived.[25]

Perkins divided the section on the uses of the resurrection into
two parts. First, he wrote about what it taught regarding Christ.
In this section he repeated some of his earlier points about the
resurrection providing proof that Jesus was the Son of God and
the saviour of the world. It also proved he was 'a perfect priest'
and that in his death he made 'perfect satisfaction to the justice
of God for the sins of mankind', because, if Christ had not fully
paid the debt for sin, if there was only one sin 'for which he had
made no satisfaction', he would not have risen. Since he did rise
again it is proof that 'he hath made so full a satisfaction that the
merit thereof doth and shall countervail the justice of God of all
our offences.'[26]

Perkins specifically listed comfort as the second use of the
resurrection. In fact, three types of comfort could be derived
from the doctrine of the resurrection. First, since Christ died and
rose in our stead 'it comes to pass, that all those which put their
trust and affiance in the merit of Christ, at the very first instant
of their believing have their own sins not imputed unto them,
and his righteousness is imputed.'[27] Second, the resurrection
serves to work for our sanctification. 'Christ being the
resurrection and the life . . . so every member of his . . . is raised
up from him and liveth unto God.'[28] However, sanctification is a
gradual process. In what should certainly have provided comfort
to those who might have been tempted to doubt their election
because they did not see sufficient evidence of their
sanctification, Perkins stated: 'We may here see most plainly,
that God worketh in the hearts of his children the gifts and
graces of regeneration by little and little. First, he giveth no more
than flesh, sinews and skin: Then after he given them further
graces of his spirit, which quickneth them and maketh them
alive unto God . . . So the Lord conveyeth his graces by little and
little, till at the last men have a full measure thereof.'[29]

---

[25] Ibid. 241.
[26] Ibid. 242.
[27] Ibid.
[28] Ibid.
[29] Ibid. 243.

Finally, the resurrection provides comfort because it is proof of our own resurrection at the day of judgement. In his *Declaration of the True Manner of Knowing Christ* Perkins stated that the resurrection preserved all the blessings Christ achieved by his death and bestowed on believers. It establishes that all our spiritual enemies have been conquered so 'none shall be able to take his sheep out of his hands.' In an eloquent summary he pointed to the resurrection as a source of reassurance against all the temptations of the devil which would undermine our comfort:

> Art thou then terrified and afraid with the conscience of thy sins, with the cruelty of tyrants, the rage of the world, the pains of hell, the pangs of death, the temptations of the devil? Be not dismayed, but by thy faith rest on Christ that rose again from death to life for thee and thereby showed himself to be a rock for thee to rest on and to be the Lion of the Tribe of Judah and thus shalt thou be sure to find certain remedy against all the troubles and miseries of life and death.[30]

Perkins concluded his discussion by commenting on three 'duties' which are the result of the resurrection. First, 'since Christ rose by his own power', we must 'by his grace and in imitation of Christ rise up from our sins unto newness of life.' The resurrection provides the motivation and power for our sanctification, because the only way we can show our gratitude for the great benefits we receive from the resurrection is by living out the newness of life which Christ's resurrection makes possible:

> The virtue of Christ's resurrection and the merit of his death, are inseparable joined together and therefore he that finds not the virtue of Christ to raise him to a holy and spiritual life acceptable to God, falsely persuades himself of the merit of his death in the remission of his sins. Christ by rising put under his feet all our enemies, and led captivity captive even sin itself. It is, therefore, a shame for us to walk in the ways of sin and to make ourselves slaves and captives to it. Christ by rising from death made himself a principal leader and guide to eternal life . . . if then we believe that Christ rose from death for us, much more should our hearts tremble and we yield ourselves in subjection to him in all spiritual obedience.[31]

---

[30] Ibid. 664.
[31] Ibid. 665

Second, we are 'to labour above all things to know Christ and the virtue of his resurrection.' Even this provides comfort for the believer. Although in order to attain this, 'we must come to hear the word of God preached and taught with fear and trembling'; we can be confident that 'the Lord of his mercy, according as he hath promised, will send his spirit of grace into our hearts, to work in us an inward sense and feeling of the virtue of Christ's resurrection.' Finally, if we are raised with Christ, it is our duty to set our mind on the things that are above and not be 'wedded to this world.'[32]

3. Thomas Goodwin (1600–80)

Clearly Perkins placed a great emphasis on the resurrection and particularly stressed the comfort it provided. He was to influence the next generation of Puritans, some of whom went even beyond him in the emphasis they placed on the resurrection and the comfort which they drew from it. Thomas Goodwin was one of those people. Goodwin was an Independent and one of the leading opponents of the effort by Presbyterians at the Westminster Assembly (1643–49) to set up a Presbyterian system of Church government for the English church. He later became President of Magdalen College, Oxford, and was a prominent member of the Savoy Assembly in 1658, a meeting of leading Independent ministers which drew up the first English Congregational doctrinal statement. After the Restoration of Charles II in 1660 he served as minister to a congregation in London. He wrote extensively, producing 'twelve densely packed volumes of deep, thorough and experimental systematic thought.'[33]

Although Goodwin did not write as much about the resurrection as Perkins, he placed an even greater emphasis on its role in our justification and sanctification. He also declared it to be an essential source of assurance for the believer. Since the

---

[32] Ibid. 664–5.

[33] Blackham, 'The Pneumatology of Thomas Goodwin', 6 (this is the best recent study of Goodwin's theology). For an account of his life and career see J. Goodwin, *A Memoir of Dr. Thomas Goodwin*, vol 2. of the *Works of Thomas Goodwin* (12 vols.; Edinburgh: James Nichol, 1861)

work of the Holy Spirit was a central emphasis in Goodwin's theology it is not surprising that, in contrast to Perkins, Goodwin credits the Holy Spirit with raising Christ from the dead:

> When Christ was dead, who was it raised him up from the grave? Which work was so great a work, as God himself accounts it as a new begetting, or making him anew, and as it were a second conception of him, a new edition of his Son Christ . . . Now, who was the immediate cause of this new advancement, whereby he was born into the other world? The Holy Ghost: Rom. viii. 11. But if the Spirit of him that raised up Jesus from the dead dwell in you, he that raised up Christ from the dead shall also quicken your mortal bodies by his Spirit that dwelleth in you.' God by his Spirit raiseth up both Christ and us.[34]

The identity between the believer and Christ, which Goodwin emphasizes in this passage, is carried further in his discussion of justification and regeneration. Goodwin used the model of Christ as the second Adam. Just as Adam 'was reckoned as a common public person, not standing singly or alone for himself, but as representing all mankind to come of him . . . Christ was a common person, representing and standing in our stead.'[35] Therefore, what Christ did was 'as if we ourselves had done it' and what was done to him for our justification is 'reckoned as done to us.' So when Christ died we died and when he rose 'God accounts that we rose also with him.'[36] Furthermore, our justification is finally achieved in the resurrection. Goodwin clearly states, 'Christ himself was justified, and that at his resurrection.' Using a legal analogy Goodwin argues that since Christ was made sin for us he must be formally acquitted of that charge. That formal act of acquittal occurred at the resurrection:

> Now in reason when should this acquittance or justification from our sins be first given to Christ and legally pronounced on him, but when he had paid the last farthing of the debt, and made his satisfaction complete? Which was then done when he began to rise; for his lying in the grave was a part of his humiliation, and so of his satisfaction as, general orthodox divines hold. Now, therefore, when he began to rise, then ended his humiliation; and that was the first movement of his exaltation; His acquittance,

---

[34] Goodwin, *Works*, vol. 6, 12–13.
[35] Goodwin, *Works*, vol. 4, 31.
[36] Ibid. 33.

therefore, bears date from thence, even from that very hour . . . Now, because he was quickened or raised by the power of the Godhead, and at that raising him he was justified also by God, and declared justified by that resurrection, as he had been declared condemned by his death; hence to be justified is put for his resurrection; for that was his justification, to declaration of all the world, that he was justified from all the sins laid to his charge.[37]

Since Christ acted in our stead, it follows 'that the persons of all the elect believers have been justified before God in Christ, as their head, at, or from the time of his resurrection.'[38]

Not only was our justification achieved in the resurrection, but Goodwin argues that it is 'the virtual cause of regeneration.' Goodwin placed a particularly strong emphasis on regeneration and the work of the Holy Spirit.[39] Both regeneration and the gift of the Holy Spirit are the result of the resurrection. Admitting that 'the dependence between Christ's resurrection and the new birth is the most difficult to discern', Goodwin developed a complex argument citing Acts 13:33, Psalm 22 and Hebrews 1:5–6 to show that just as Christ's 'resurrection is called his begetting again, so our resurrection is called our regeneration.'[40]

He also connected the resurrection with baptism, citing Colossians 2:12 and 1 Peter 3:21 to contend that 'Baptism is the sacrament of regeneration; and when the apostle says "baptism saves," his meaning is that the grace in baptism which is regeneration (for that is the thing sealed up) wrought by Christ's resurrection doth save us.'[41] Whereas all Christ's works have an impact on us, some things are attributed more to a specific event. Thus 'the begetting or infusing a new principle of life into us' is specifically attributed to the resurrection in Romans 6:5. The new birth is connected with the resurrection because Christ's resurrection 'was the entrance and first step into his gloried condition' and through it he sent the Holy Spirit to begin

---

[37] Ibid. 36.
[38] Ibid. 37.
[39] Blackham, 'The Pneumatology of Thomas Goodwin', 207.
[40] Goodwin, *Works*, vol. 6, 455.
[41] Ibid. 456.

the work of regeneration in us. Goodwin summed up his argument on the connection between the resurrection, regeneration and baptism in the following words:

> Christ's resurrection is the exemplary cause of our regeneration, according to which, the Spirit, or that same power that wrought in him, works a work in us conformable to his resurrection . . . And thus our begetting again (which is by the infusion of a new life) bears the image of Christ's resurrection, and so is attributed unto it . . . Now baptism is the sacrament of regeneration, which resembles, in the dipping under water and coming forth again, our burial with Christ in his grave, and our rising again by faith and a new life: Col ii. 12 . . . As the resurrection of Christ was the great 'declaration of him to be the Son of God, with power, Rom. i. 4; so is the regeneration of a believer the first declaration of his being a son of God, and the first discovery of his election . . . As Christ's resurrection was the first step unto his glory, and to that exhaltation that followed his resurrection, so regeneration is the foundation and first step unto all those privileges of a Christian that follow upon the state of grace whereunto this is the door or first entrance.'[42]

Goodwin also considered the resurrection a ground of assurance for the believer. Returning again to the connection between baptism and the resurrection, he maintained that when our sins condemn or accuse us we can turn to our communion with Christ in his resurrection represented in our baptism and argue 'Christ is risen, and I was then justified in him. There is my answer, which nothing in heaven or hell is able to reply unto. This is the answer of a good conscience, by the resurrection of Jesus Christ.'[43] Goodwin ended his discussion of the way in which Christ's resurrection provides assurance to the believer with a marvellous application of his resurrection theology. Responding to the problem which plagued so many Puritans – how do I know that I am one of those for whom Christ died? – he stated:

> And should thy heart object and say, But I know not whether I was one of those that God reckoned justified with Christ when he arose; then go thou to God, and ask him boldly, whether he did not do this for thee, and God will (by virtue of Christ's

---

[42] Ibid. 457–8.
[43] Goodwin, *Works*, vol. 7, 42.

resurrection for thee) even himself answer thy faith this question
ere thou art aware. He will not deny it. And to secure the more,
know that however Christ will be sure to look to that for thee; so
as that thou having been then intended . . . shalt never be
condemned.[44]

4. Stephen Charnock (1628–80)

Just as Goodwin concluded his discussion of the resurrection
with a resounding word of comfort, so Stephen Charnock also
stressed the comfort which believers find in the doctrine of the
resurrection. Charnock was a member of Goodwin's
independent church meeting in Oxford during the Protectorate
and seems to have been influenced by Goodwin's thought. After
15 years without a ministry during the Restoration, in 1675 he
was appointed joint rector, with Thomas Watson, of an
important Presbyterian Congregation which met in Crosby Hall,
Bishopsgates, London. By that time his memory and his eyesight
were failing and he was forced to read his sermons with a
magnifying glass. James McCosh, who wrote the biographical
introduction to the 1866 edition of his works, states that 'his
bodily infirmities, his trials and spiritual conflicts gave him a
peculiar fitness for guiding the anxious and comforting the
afflicted', so it is not surprising that his comments on the
resurrection centre on the comfort that Christians can find in
that doctrine.[45]

In a fashion reminiscent of Goodwin, Charnock relied heavily
on legal terminology in his description of what happened in the
resurrection. In *Discourse on the Acceptableness of Christ's
Death*, based on Ephesians 5:2, he presented the resurrection in
legal terms as the evidence that Christ had been acquitted. He
called the resurrection 'clear evidence' of the sufficiency of
Christ's sacrifice for us:

He was not totally swallowed up by divine justice, but
surmounted all the strokes of it and lifted up his head above the

---

[44] Ibid. 43.
[45] J. McCosh, 'Introduction', *The Complete Works of Stephen Charnock*, vol. 1,
xiv.

waves that surrounded him. The fetters of death had not been unlocked, if his sacrifice had not been satisfactory . . . This raising him was a justification of him, for when he was taken from prison he was taken from judgement also, that no suits could be brought against him, or any new actions laid upon him; and he was declared to be the Son of God and he was declared to be so 'with power.'[46]

In his *Discourse of God Being the Author of Reconciliation*, he again reverted to legal analogies, stating that the resurrection established that 'the controversy between God and sinners upon the account of the law was at an end, and the bond was cancelled in token of full satisfaction.'[47]

In contrast to Perkins and Goodwin, Charnock maintained that the resurrection was primarily an act of the Father. Referring to Romans 6:4, he argued that 'the body of Christ was raised, and resurrection is not the work of either soul or body, but of God only. God raised him from the dead in such a manner as to declare him to be his Son.' Although he acknowledged that the resurrection was in fact the work of the entire Trinity, since 1 Peter 3:18 teaches that he was 'quickened by the Spirit' and in the Gospel of John, Christ is also said to have raised himself, nevertheless, 'acts of power are more peculiarly ascribed to the Father and resurrection is an act of omnipotence, as wisdom is ascribed to the Son and love to the Holy Ghost.'[48] He pointed out that it was fitting for the Father to have the principal role in the resurrection because 'the Father had the power of mission, and therefore of acceptation; and therefore the act whereby it was declared did principally pertain to the Father, as it was a full manifestation of the faithfulness of Christ in his office.'[49] Returning again to the legal analogies he commented: 'as the Father was the lawgiver and judge, the delivering Christ to death belonged to him; upon the same account the delivering him from prison and judgement belonged to the Father.'[50]

Most of Charnock's comments on the resurrection emphasized the comfort which it brings to the believer. He maintained that it brings 'us the highest security for all new

[46] Charnock, *Works*, vol. 4, 559.
[47] Charnock, *Works*, vol. 3, 435.
[48] Ibid. 436.
[49] Ibid.
[50] Charnock, *Works*, vol. 3, 437.

covenant mercies', because there can be no greater security than fulfilment of promises made and in the resurrection God's promises are fulfilled:

> The wisdom of God, the righteousness of God, and the truth of God, did all shine forth in their fullest beams, in the raising him from the dead, which was the top-stone of our reconciliation, as his death had been the corner-stone and foundation. The certain enjoyment of all the blessings of the new covenant is insured to us by this act of God, and so intended by him in the act itself . . . How strong a ground is here for our faith and comfort! . . . Peace dawned at his birth, but was not in its meridian till his resurrection ... we should go to him as a God of peace, as a God lifting up Christ from the grave, that he might with honour to all his attributes work such excellent things in the hearts of all that believe in him . . . [51]

Charnock's most extensive discussion of the resurrection is found in his *Discourse on the Necessity of Christ's Exaltation*. Most of that discussion is once again devoted to the comfort which comes to the believer through the resurrection. Christ's resurrection is described as the beginning of his exaltation which is fully achieved in his ascension. 'In Christ's death, the nature of his sacrifice is declared; in his resurrection, the validity and perfection of this sacrifice is manifested; in his glorious ascension, the everlasting virtue of that sacrifice is testified.'[52]

Christ is now our advocate in heaven and his resurrection is 'an assurance that the same power should be employed for doing all works necessary in a justified person.' Consequently, we have 'assurance from hence of a holy assistance in and an honourable success of all afflictions and temptations.'[53] The resurrection is also the assurance of our resurrection. The exhaltation of the head means that the rest of the body will follow. Charnock calls it 'the seal and earnest and infallible argument of it', and he describes the resurrection as 'a pledge of the advancement of believers in their persons, and a transporting them from this vale of misery to the heavenly sanctuary.'[54]

---

[51] Ibid. 438–9.
[52] Charnock, *Works*, vol. 5, 83.
[53] Ibid. 84–5.
[54] Ibid. 87.

5. Thomas Manton (1620–77)

Thomas Manton was a contemporary of Charnock and Goodwin. He was the acknowledged leader of the Presbyterians in London during the 1640s and one of the three scribes for the Westminster Assembly. He also served as one of the 'triers' of godly ministers during the Protectorate (1653–59). Along with Richard Baxter he was one of the moderate Presbyterians who tried to work out an accommodation with the Church of England. He was one of the deputation who went to Breda to arrange the Restoration, he sat on the commission for the revision of liturgy and attended the Savoy Conference which attempted to arrive at an agreement between Puritans and Anglicans. When the effort failed, he held services in his own home in Covent Garden. In 1670 he was arrested and imprisoned for six months, but he continued to work with Baxter for a comprehensive Church of England which would be broad enough to include Puritans. He was a popular preacher and much of his 22 volumes of published works consists of sermons which include a substantial number of sermons on the resurrection.

Manton differed from the other writers we have considered with his balanced Trinitarian approach to the resurrection. Whereas Perkins has emphasized the Son, Goodwin the Holy Spirit and Charnock the Father, Manton argued that all three persons in the Trinity played an equal role in the resurrection, since it was a work of 'divine power' which 'belongeth in common to Father, Son and Holy Ghost, who being one and the same God, concurred in the same work.'[55] Manton supported his analysis with biblical references which the other writers had also cited, but he used them in a more balanced way maintaining that the Bible ascribed Christ's resurrection to all three persons of the Trinity co-equally:

> It is ascribed to God the Father, who in the mystery of redemption hath the relation of supreme judge: Acts ii. 32 'This Jesus hath God raised up: and Acts x. 40, 'Him hath God raised up the third day.' And there is a special reason why it should be ascribed to

---

[55] T. Manton, *The Complete Works of Thomas Manton* (22 vols; Worthington, PA: Maranatha, n.d.), vol. 12, 20.

God, as the Apostles when they stood upon their privilege, 'Let them come and fetch us out,' Acts xii. 39; so 'The God of peace that brought again from the dead the great shepherd,' etc., as referring it to his judicial power: Heb. xiii. 26. Though Christ had power to rise, yet no authority; our surety was fetched out of prison by the judge. And then it is ascribed to Christ himself: John ii. 19, 'Destroy this temple, and in three days I will raise it up: which he spake of the temple of his body.' To prove the divinity of his person, it was necessary that he should thus speak; or to prove himself to be God: John x.18, 'I have power to lay down my life, and to take it up again.' He could put a period to his sufferings when he pleased. So for the Holy Ghost, he raised Christ, because the Spirit sanctified his humanity, and by him the human nature of Christ was made partaker of created holiness, and so qualified to rise again when he had done his work.[56]

It would be hard to find a writer who places a greater stress on the resurrection than Manton. He called the resurrection 'the great prop and foundation of our faith' maintaining it was 'the corner-stone in religion, the main hinge upon which gospel comfort hangs.'[57] It had a major role in justification and sanctification as well as providing 'the chiefest ground of comfort to Christians in the scripture.'[58] Manton maintained that Scripture taught that 'there is some special thing in Christ's resurrection comparatively above his death, which hath an influence upon our justification.'[59] That role included proof that Christ was the son of God and that Christ's sacrifice was sufficient to pay the debt for our sins since 'if Christ had been an impostor or false prophet, neither could he have raised up himself being a mere man, nor would God have raised him up if he had been a mere deceiver.' The resurrection was also 'a token of the acceptance of his purchase, or a solemn aquittance, a full discharge of Christ as our mediator and surety' which showed 'God hath received the death of Christ as a sufficient ransom for our sins.' In his resurrection Christ was given 'a capacity to convey life to others, which, if he had remained in a state of death he could not do.'[60]

---

[56] Ibid. 21.
[57] Manton, *Works*, vol. 1, 473.
[58] Manton, *Works*, vol. 3, 349.
[59] Manton, *Works*, vol. 12, 368.
[60] Ibid. 370.

Manton particularly emphasized the role the resurrection played in sanctification and in providing comfort for Christians. The resurrection first provided the power to live the new life in Christ: 'One great point or part of the experimental knowledge of Christ is knowing the power of his resurrection . . . This power is the Lord's work in regeneration whereby he bestoweth upon us a new life, a spiritual life of grace . . . This new life is not only an obligation to live in a purity and holiness to the glory of God, but an inclination or a power to do so.'[61]

It also verifies the truth of the Christian faith and this certain proof that what we believe is true serves to encourage us in our spiritual life since 'it is a mighty advantage to the advancement of the spiritual life to be sure of the religion that requireth it at our hands' so our 'corrupt nature' cannot use the excuse of uncertainty of Christian truth to undermine our spiritual life.[62] Christ's resurrection is also a model and example for our own death to sin and our rising to new life. 'There is a great likeness and correspondence between Christ's rising from the grave, and a Christian's resurrection from the death of sin.' Just as through Christ's resurrection sin no longer has dominion over him, 'so is a Christian put into an unchangeable state: sin hath no more dominion over him . . . Though formerly dead in sin he shall live the life of grace.'[63]

The resurrection is also the major source of comfort for Christians. First, it assures them of their own resurrection. In one sermon Manton spoke of Christ's resurrection making our resurrection 'possible . . . easy, certain and necessary.' 'For all religion is bottomed on the resurrection of Christ; if, therefore, Christ be raised, why should it seem any incredible thing for us that others should be raised also? It is easy. For by rising from the dead he hath conquered death and gotten victory of it.'[64]

It also made our resurrection 'certain and necessary' because Christ as the head of the body will not live gloriously in heaven and leave his members behind him under the power of death.'[65]

---

61 Manton, *Works*, vol. 20, 59.
62 Manton, *Works*, vol. 11, 222.
63 Manton, *Works*, vol. 13, 204.
64 Manton, *Works*, vol. 1, 470.
65 Ibid. 471.

Manton's most extended comment on the resurrection is found in his *Practical Exposition upon the Fifty-Third Chapter of Isaiah*. He devoted over ten pages to commenting on why Christ was raised from the dead. Throughout he stressed the comfort Christians can find in the resurrection. He began by stating that the resurrection was an answer to Christ's prayer in the garden. 'He did not so much pray that he might not die, as that he might be saved from death; that having taken so much guilt upon him, he might not sink under it' and his Father 'whose tenderness would not let him leave Christ in the grave, nor suffer his Holy One to see corruption' answered that prayer.[66]

Manton continued with an analysis of God's purposes in raising Christ. He stated that it was meant to be for believers 'the fountain of their comfort . . . since all the comfort of the soul dependeth upon his getting above the grave and shaking the powers of death.'[67] After reviewing the benefits which believers derive from the resurrection in which 'all spiritual blessings are procured for us' including justification, 'sanctification' and eventually 'glorification', Manton asked what may seem to us a redundant question: 'What is it that it [the resurrection] contributes to the comfort of Christians above his death?'[68] This provided him with an opportunity to review how the resurrection proves the divinity of Christ, confirms that as our mediator Christ has made full satisfaction for our sins, and serves as a pledge of our own resurrection.

Although one might assume Manton had said enough to illustrate how the resurrection should bring comfort and consolation to the believer, he had still more to add. He concluded his comments by discussing the use of the doctrine of the resurrection. Beginning with the comment, 'Christians, here is comfort for the saddest believer', Manton used the same type of arguments Puritans included in their tracts on assurance to illustrate how Christian assurance could be found in the

---

[66] Manton, *Works*, vol. 3, 348. Even though Manton at this point attributed the resurrection to the Father he quickly added that Christ also raised himself and that 'His resurrection was glorious instance and manifestation of his own Godhead', 349.

[67] Ibid.

[68] Manton, *Works*, vol. 3, 351.

resurrection.[69] In a classic passage which illustrates his emphasis on the resurrection as a source of assurance for the despondent and distressed believer who may have begun to doubt his salvation he wrote:

> There is no misery but some passage of Christ's life is parallel to it. Out of all these considerations you may fetch a great deal of comfort. Reason then against all the depths of misery into which you may be cast; I shall get free, for Christ got free; I see the success in the story of Christ's life. Is it the depth of inward misery? Ps. xviii. 5, 'The sorrows of hell compassed me about, and the snares of death compassed me.' So they did Christ, yet he got free of them, as the apostle saith, Heb. xii. 2, 'Looking unto Jesus, the author and finisher of our faith, who for the joy that was set before him endured the cross, despising the shame, and is set down at the right hand of the throne of God.' Is it outward misery? None could have more distress upon him than Christ, yet he was taken from distress and judgement. Is it death? Christ died and rose again. Either God will preserve you from the evil, or he will order it so that it shall not hold you.[70]

Manton concluded his discussion by assuring his readers 'true believers cannot wholly fall away. Christ liveth forever, and, therefore, they shall live for ever; the life of Christ cannot wholly be abolished in them.'[71]

6. Conclusion

Perkins, Goodwin, Charnock and Manton all placed a great emphasis on the resurrection, and, if we are correct in assuming that their teaching reflects a wider consensus among Puritans, it is clear that the resurrection of Jesus was a central concern in Puritan thought and especially in their pastoral theology. Although the four differed in their beliefs about which person in the Godhead had the major role in the resurrection, and they had different emphases as well as different ways of presenting

---

[69] See J. Beeke, 'Personal Assurance of Faith: the Puritans and Chapter 18.2 of the Westminster Confession', *Westminster Theological Journal* 55 (1993), 1–30 for a useful brief discussion of Puritan teaching on assurance.

[70] Manton, *Works*, vol. 3, 357.

[71] Ibid. 359.

their teaching, they were in fundamental agreement on most points. All believed that the resurrection played a major role in our justification and sanctification and that it was a prime source of comfort and reassurance to the believer. Puritan teaching on the resurrection seems also to have been used partly to confront the problem of doubt and despair which Wallington experienced and which writers like Worden and Stachniewski maintain resulted from Puritan theology.

That emphasis on the comfort and reassurance to be found in the resurrection is especially evident in the pastoral theology of Richard Baxter. As minister at Kidderminster from 1641–60 Baxter provided a model for Christian ministry. He was also one of the leading spokesmen for a moderate Puritanism during the Civil War period. He drew up the revision of the Book of Common Prayer which was rejected at the Savoy Conference and suffered greatly as a result of the Restoration settlement. He left more that 200 writings in which he addressed some of the most sensitive issues confronting Purtians. Few people were more aware of the despair that could result from the desperate search for assurance of one's election than Baxter. He had experienced those struggles personally and in 1671 he wrote a book entitled *God's Goodness Vindicated* in which he attempted to deal with some of the problems occasioned by the theological emphasis which resulted in such despair. Although Baxter did not discuss the resurrection in that work, in his *Treatise of Death* he pointed to the resurrection as the greatest source of assurance for Christians, making it possible to 'answer a thousand cavils of the tempter, and stop the mouth of the enemies of our faith, and put to flight our infidelity.' The importance of the resurrection in Puritan thought and the joy with which they celebrated Christ's victory over death could hardly be expressed more fervently than in the following words of Baxter, which provide a fitting conclusion to this study:

> No wonder . . . that the church, in all ages, ever since the very day of Christ's resurrection, hath kept the first day of the week as a holy festival in remembrance of it. Wherein, though they commemorated the whole work of our redemption, yet was it from the resurrection as the most glorious part that the Spirit of Christ did choose the day. This hath been the joyful day to the church this 1625 years, or thereabouts; in which the ancient

Christians would assemble themselves together, saluting one another with this joyful word, 'The Lord is risen.' And this is the day that the Lord hath blessed with the new birth and resurrection of millions of souls; so that it is most probably that all the six days of the week have not begot half so many souls for heaven, as this blessed day of the Lord's resurrection hath done. Let infidels, then, despise it, that believe not Christ's resurrection; but let it still be the church's joyful day. This is the Lord's doing; it is marvellous in our eyes: this is the day the Lord hath made, we will rejoice and be glad in it.[72]

Questions for further study

1. Did the Puritan writers considered in this study make a useful contribution to our understanding of the resurrection and its application to Christian living?

2. What do Perkins, Goodwin, Charnock and Manton have in common in their teaching about the resurrection? How do they differ?

3. Why did Perkins, Goodwin, Charnock and Manton consider the resurrection such a central doctrine of the faith?

4. In your opinion did Puritan teaching on the resurrection provide an adequate answer to the problem of doubt and despair which writers like Worden and Stachniewski maintain resulted from Puritan theology?

5. How does Puritan teaching on the resurrection compare with biblical teaching in Luke–Acts and Romans?

6. How can we apply Puritan thought on the resurrection to our lives and ministries?

---

[72] R. Baxter, *The Practical Works of Richard Baxter* (London: James Duncan, 1830), vol. 17, 588–9.

Select Bibliography

Collections of primary works have been cited throughout in the notes and should be available in good theological libraries. The following books provide a useful introduction to English Puritan thought.

Collinson, P., *The Elizabethan Puritan Movement* (Oxford: Clarendon, 1989)

Durston, C. & Eales, J. (eds.), *The Culture of English Puritanism 1560–1700* (London: Macmillan, 1996)

Packer, J.I., *Among God's Giants: Aspects of Puritan Christianity* (Eastbourne: Kingsway, 1991)

Ryken, L., *Worldly Saints* (Grand Rapids: Zondervan, 1986)

Watkins, O., *The Puritan Experience* (London: Routledge & Kegan Paul, 1972)

Five

The Resurrection of Jesus Christ in the Theology of Karl Barth

MARTIN DAVIE

1. Introduction

In his lectures on *Evangelical Theology* Karl Barth himself rejects the idea that there is any such thing as a 'great' theologian. As he sees it, all theologians are 'little theologians', men and women who are overwhelmed by the greatness of the God with whom they have to do.[1]

Nevertheless, in human terms Barth ranks as a great theologian. In fact, most commentators have agreed that he was probably the twentieth century's greatest theologian. As S. J. Grenz and R. E. Olson observe:

> When future historians of theology look back on the twentieth century there is little doubt who they will name as its single most influential Christian thinker: Karl Barth. Widely recognised during his own lifetime as a modern Christian father, he is often classed with Augustine, Aquinas, Luther and Schleiermacher because of his massive, original contribution to theology. Virtually

---

[1] K. Barth, *Evangelical Theology* (London/Glasgow: Fontana, 1963), 74-5.

all twentieth century theologians have sensed a need to respond to him in some way.[2]

However, although Barth has thus been widely accepted as a great theologian, which is why it is worth our while to listen to what he has to say about the resurrection, he remains an extremely controversial one since the theological ideas he developed challenge both liberal and conservative Christians alike. His teaching on the resurrection illustrates this very clearly. On the one hand he insists, against much liberal thought, that the bodily resurrection of Christ lies at the very heart of the Christian message. On the other hand, unlike many conservative writers, he is sceptical about detailed historical accuracy of the New Testament accounts of the resurrection appearances and does not accept that they can be used to provide historical evidence for the truth of the resurrection.

In this paper I want to explore these two contrasting aspects of Barth's teaching, looking at why Barth is so insistent on the bodily nature of the resurrection, what he thinks the theological importance of the resurrection is, and also asking why he is nevertheless sceptical about the historical nature of the New Testament accounts. Finally, I shall attempt an assessment of the value of Barth's thought in this area for us today.

2. The bodily nature of the resurrection

In his important book *Space, Time and Resurrection* the Scottish theologian T.F. Torrance records that in his final conversation with Barth a few weeks before Barth's death he suggested to Barth that '. . . it might be only too easy, judging from many of our contemporaries and even some of his former students, to think of the resurrection after all in a rather docetic way, lacking concrete ontological reality. But at that remark, Barth leaned over to me and said with considerable force, which I shall never forget, *"Wohlverstanden, leibliche Auferstehung"* – "Mark well, bodily resurrection".'[3]

---

[2] S.J. Grenz and R.E. Olson, *20th Century Theology: God and the World in a transitional age* (Exeter: Paternoster, 1992), 65.

[3] T.F. Torrance, *Space, Time and Resurrection* (Edinburgh: Handsel, 1976), xi.

This remark of Barth's cannot be seen as simply a one-off. There is abundant evidence that in his mature thought Barth was convinced of the importance of the bodily nature of the resurrection and the significance of the empty tomb as its sign. Three examples will serve to substantiate this point.

In his 1935 lectures on the *Apostles' Creed*, entitled *Credo*, Barth writes:

> The miracle consists in the two facts that belong together and that, at least in the opinion of all the New Testament witnesses, are not explicable on the assumption of fraud and deception or by the possibility of a mere vision – the one, that the *grave* of that Jesus who died on the Cross on Good Friday was found *empty* on the third day, the other that Jesus 'appears' as the characteristic expression puts it, to his disciples as visibly, audibly, tangibly alive. The concrete content of the memory of the forty days is: Christ is risen, He is risen indeed! To be exegetically accurate we must understand by this 'indeed' corporeally risen; and thus, if we are not to make so bold as to substitute for the apostolic witness another one altogether, there cannot be any talk of striking out the empty grave.[4]

Second, in his 1947 lectures on the *Heidelberg Catechism* at the University of Bonn, Barth explicitly rejects the suggestion by the German New Testament scholar Rudolf Bultmann that the resurrection accounts in the New Testament really refer to the rise of faith in the disciples. He insists instead that the resurrection of Christ was a real, objective event in space and time:

> The conquest of death and the exaltation of life was an event in Jesus Christ the head. His exaltation is history just as his humiliation is history. For this reason we must simply say No to Bultmann's 'demythologization' of the New Testament. The 'resurrection of Jesus Christ' means the resurrection of this one person in space and time just like the event of Golgotha. If it does not mean that, this event is reduced to a new determination of human existence, to the awakening of faith in the first disciples. Then there is no Christ for us and over us to substantiate the existence of Christ in us. Then the Easter message as such is subverted and nullified.[5]

---

[4] *Credo* (London: Hodder & Stoughton, 1964), 100.
[5] *Learning Jesus Christ through the Heidelberg Catechism* (Grand Rapids: Eerdmans, 1964), 75–6.

Third, in *Church Dogmatics* III/2, first published in 1948, Barth argues that if we are to avoid docetism and affirm that the risen Jesus was truly human then we cannot gloss over the bodily character of the resurrection appearances: 'We misunderstand the whole matter and fall into docetism at the crucial point if we refuse to see this and even see it first. . . It is the fact that the risen Christ can be touched which puts it beyond all doubt that He is the man Jesus and no one else. He is not soul or body in the abstract, but soul of His body, and therefore body as well.'[6]

In fact, according to Barth, the physical nature of Christ's resurrection is so important that

> To be an apostle of Jesus Christ means not only to have seen him with one's eyes and to have heard Him with one's ears, but to have touched Him physically. This is what is meant by Acts 1:22, where we are told that what makes an apostle is the fact that he is a 'witness of the resurrection.' By beholding His glory, by seeing, hearing and touching the flesh in which this glory is made manifest, those who consorted with Jesus during this time were brought to believe in Him, and thus authorised and consecrated to proclaim the Gospel. 'Blessed are they that have not seen, and yet have believed' (Jn. 20:29). This is not a criticism of Thomas, but (cf. 1 Pet. 1:8) the blessing of all those who, though having no part in the seeing of this particular time, will 'believe on me through their word,' i.e., through the witness of those who did see (Jn. 17:20).[7]

It is, says Barth,

> . . . impossible to erase the bodily character of the resurrection of Jesus and His existence as the Resurrected. Nor may we gloss over this element in the New Testament record of the forty days, as a false dualism between spirit and body has repeatedly tried to do. For unless Christ's resurrection was a resurrection of the body, we have no guarantee that it was decisively the acting Subject Jesus Himself, the *man* Jesus, who rose from the dead.[8]

Not only does Barth thus insist on the physicality of the resurrection, but in this same section of *Church Dogmatics* III/2 he also asserts that the empty tomb, like the ascension, is an

---

[6] *Church Dogmatics* (Edinburgh: T.&T. Clark, 1960), vol. III/2, 448.
[7] Ibid.
[8] Ibid.

indispensable sign of the reality of the resurrection itself. Barth agrees that the empty tomb is not the centre of the Easter message:

> The content of the Easter witness, the Easter event, was not that they found the tomb empty or that they saw him go up to heaven, but that when they had lost Him through death they were sought and found by Him as the Resurrected. The empty tomb and the ascension are merely signs of the Easter event, just as the Virgin Birth is merely the sign of the nativity, namely of the human generation and birth of the eternal Son of God.[9]

Yet, he says, although the empty tomb and the ascension are but signs: 'both signs are so important that we can hardly say that they might equally well be omitted.'[10] In his view, the function of the empty tomb as a sign is '. . . to show that the Jesus who died and was buried was delivered from death, and therefore from the grave, by the power of God; that He, the living, is not to be sought among the dead (Lk. 24:5). 'He is risen; he is not here: behold the place where they laid him' (Mk. 16:6). 'He is not here; for he is risen, even as he said' (Mt. 28:6, Lk. 24:6). He is not here!'[11]

Referring to Mt. 27:62f. and 28:11f., Barth notes, as many others have done, that 'the empty tomb was obviously a very ambiguous and contestable fact.' He also notes that 'It is not the appearance of the Living; it is only its presupposition', and that 'Christians do not believe in the empty tomb, but in the living Christ.'[12]

However, this having been said, he still maintains that this 'does not mean, however, that we can believe in the living Christ without believing in the empty tomb.' This is because, for Barth, the empty tomb is 'the sign which obviates all possible misunderstanding', and 'Rejection of the legend of the empty tomb has always been accompanied by rejection of the saga of the living Jesus.'[13]

Later on in this paper we shall consider Barth's use of the problematic terms 'legend' and 'saga.' For the moment, however,

---

[9] Ibid. 453.
[10] Ibid.
[11] Ibid.
[12] Ibid.
[13] Ibid.

the point to note is that Barth clearly and unambiguously confirms the necessity of believing in both the physical resurrection of Jesus Christ and the empty tomb as its accompanying sign. For him the Easter affirmation that Christ is risen indeed means the affirmation that He was raised bodily and that in consequence His tomb was empty. According to Barth we have to affirm this if

1. We are to be faithful to the New Testament witness.

2. We are to avoid identifying the risen Christ with our subjective religious experience as he feels Bultmann does.

3. We are to avoid docetism and maintain the risen Christ's true humanity.

3. The theological significance of the resurrection

It would however be misleading to suggest that the main concern of Barth's teaching on the resurrection was to defend its physical nature. As we shall see in more detail later in this paper, Barth was not a Swiss Michael Green or Frank Morison seeking to convince a sceptical world that the resurrection really happened. The primary purpose of Barth's writing on the resurrection was, instead, to explain its theological significance and it is to his explanation of its significance that we shall now turn.

The revelation of Jesus' identity

The first point of significance that Barth attaches to the resurrection is that it is the point in history at which Jesus' true identity as incarnate God is revealed to us. This is a point that is made by Barth very early on in his career in his seminal commentary on *The Epistle to the Romans* in which the question of how human beings can have an authentic knowledge of God is a major theme. Commenting on Paul's words in Romans 1:4, 'declared to be the Son of God with power, according to the Holy Spirit, through his resurrection from the dead', Barth writes:

> As the Christ, He brings the world of the Father. But we who stand in this concrete world know nothing, and are incapable of

knowing anything of that other world. The Resurrection from the dead is, however, the transformation: the establishing or *declaration* of that point from above, and the corresponding discerning of it from below. The Resurrection is the revelation: the disclosing of Jesus as the Christ, the appearing of God, and the apprehending of God in Jesus.[14]

This idea of the resurrection as the point at which Jesus' identity is revealed is then subsequently developed in the *Church Dogmatics*. Thus Barth declares: 'The resurrection is meant when it says in Jn. 1:14: 'We saw his glory.' The resurrection is the event of the revelation of the Incarnate, the Humiliated, the Crucified. Wherever He gives Himself to be known as the person He is, He speaks as the risen Christ. The resurrection can give nothing new to Him who is the eternal Word of the Father; but it makes visible what is proper to Him, His glory.'[15]

Most clearly and unequivocally of all, Barth argues that just as during the forty days after the resurrection Jesus was present with His disciples as a true human being (a point we have already noted) so also He was present with them during this time in unveiled deity. It is, he says,

> ... equally important to note that the man Jesus appeared to them during these days in the mode of God. During this period they came to see that He had always been present among them in His deity, though hitherto this deity had been veiled. They now recalled these preliminary manifestations of glory which they had already witnessed during his earthly life, but with unseeing eyes, and which now, in the light of what happened in those days, acquired for them the particular import which they had always had in themselves, though hidden from them. Now they actually beheld His glory.[16]

According to Barth:

> During these forty days the presence of God in the presence of the man Jesus was no longer a paradox. The dialectic of seeing and believing may be helpful when we try to describe the Christian life and the justification and sanctification of Christians, or the Church and its preaching and sacraments. But when we come to

---

[14] *The Epistle to the Romans* (Oxford: OUP, 1968), 30.
[15] *Church Dogmatics* (Edinburgh: T.&T. Clark, 1980), vol. I/2, 111.
[16] *Church Dogmatics*, vol. III/2, 448–9.

the resurrection it leads us nowhere. 'God was in Christ' (2 Cor. 5:19) – this was the truth which dawned upon the disciples during the forty days. He was not both veiled and manifest, both manifest and veiled in Christ. He had been veiled, but He was now wholly and unequivocally and irrevocably manifest.[17]

The resurrection is thus the point at which the unbelief of the disciples is decisively overcome. Barth notes that in the resurrection narratives 'the disciples begin by doubting and even disbelieving.' But, he says,

> . . . their doubts and disbelief are soon dispelled, never to return. They are definitively overcome and removed in the forty days. 'Be not faithless, but believing' (John 20:27f.) This is not just pious exhortation, but a word of power. And to this Thomas gives the appropriate answer: 'My Lord and my God.' In and with the presence of the man Jesus during this time, in the unique circumstances of the forty days, a decision is taken between the belief and unbelief of His disciples. There takes place for them the total, final, irrevocable and eternal manifestation of God Himself. God Himself, the object and ground of their faith, was present as the man Jesus was present in this way.[18]

For Barth, therefore, God reveals Himself clearly and unambiguously in the person of the resurrected Christ. This then raises the question of what God reveals about Himself in this way. Barth's threefold answer to this question is given as follows:

> He was thus the concrete demonstration of the gracious God, who in the death of this man on the cross did not will that His own right, and that of man, should go by default, but willed to vindicate them, as He did in great triumph. He was then the concrete demonstration of the God who not only has authority over man's life and death, but also wills to deliver him from death. Moreover . . . He was the concrete demonstration of the God who has not only a different time from that of man, but whose will and resolve it is to give man a share in this time of His, in His eternity. The concrete demonstration of this God, His appearance, is the meaning of the appearance and appearances of this man Jesus, alive again after his death, in the forty days.[19]

---

[17] Ibid. 449.
[18] Ibid.
[19] Ibid. 450-1.

The fulfilment of the cross

Taking each of the points Barth makes in this important passage in turn, the first point to note is that, according to Karl Barth, the resurrection reveals the gracious nature of God's activity in the cross of Jesus Christ. Once again, this is an idea that Barth first puts forward in *The Epistle to the Romans* and then develops in his later works.

In *The Epistle to the Romans* Barth responds to Paul's words, 'But if we died with Christ, we believe that we shall also live with him' (Rom. 6:8), by asking, 'What then, we ask is that in which we believe? We believe that Christ died in our place, and that therefore we died with him. We believe in our identity with the invisible new man who stands on the other side of the Cross. We believe in the eternal existence of ours which is grounded upon the knowledge of death, upon the resurrection, upon God.' [20]

If we unpack this dense statement, what Barth is saying is that our faith as Christians rests upon our knowledge of God's act in the cross and resurrection in which our old sinful nature was done to death and a new nature given to us in its place.

This concept of the resurrection as the fulfilment of God's saving activity on the cross is at the heart of Barth's understanding of the atonement. For him the meaning of the cross is not so much that Christ paid the penalty for sin so that we do not have to, but that, as Paul teaches in 2 Corinthians 5:14, in the death of Christ the annihilating judgement of God was enacted upon sinful humanity so that our old nature might be destroyed *in order that* it might be replaced by the new nature made manifest to us in Christ by His resurrection on the third day.

Thus in his lectures on the *Heidelberg Catechism* Barth declares:

> Redemption through righteousness means an *act of judgement* in which the right of man is restored as a consequence of the fact that the right of God is re-established. This happens in the resurrection and ascension of Jesus Christ, in his *status exultationis*, his state of exaltation. This is the gospel of Easter, the *theologia gloriae*, theology of glory. The revealed word of God says

---

[20] *The Epistle to the Romans*, 202.

both things: cross and resurrection, lowliness and majesty, of the true Son of God and Son of man.

In the death of Jesus Christ, God took man's place in order to suffer in his place the destruction of sinful man and, at the same time, to realize the existence of the new obedient man. The way is therefore open to restore the lost right of man, his right to live as the creature of God. The grace of God against which man sins triumphs in Jesus Christ.[21]

What Barth is saying here is that the cross and the resurrection together are an act of divine judgement in which, through the destruction of sinful humanity and its replacement by a new obedient humanity, both God's right to be the God of an obedient people and our right to live as His obedient creatures are re-established and restored.

He makes the same point even more precisely in a section in *Church Dogmatics* in which he considers the nature of the relationship between the cross and the resurrection as the 'two acts of the one history of God with a sinful and corrupt world.' In this section he begins by stating that 'According to the resurrection the death of Jesus Christ as the negative act of God took place with a positive intention.'[22]

If we ask what this aim was, Barth's answer is that the fulfilment of the cross by the resurrection shows that it was '. . . the turning of man to Himself, his positing afresh, his putting on a new life, his freeing for the future.'[23]

Conversely, he argues that we can see that the resurrection fulfils the destructive purpose of the cross through '. . . a radical turning of man from his old existence, in a total removing of his earlier form, in his absolute putting off, in his complete freedom from the past.'[24]

Picking up the idea of the joint right of God to be God and of Man to be His obedient creature which we have already looked at in connection with his lectures on the *Heidelberg Catechism*, Barth declares that the resurrection of Christ

---

[21] *Learning Jesus Christ through the Heidelberg Catechism*, 72-3.
[22] *Church Dogmatics*, vol. IV/1, 310.
[23] Ibid.
[24] Ibid.

. . . confirmed in what sense God was in the right in His death – not surrendering but asserting His right against sinful men who, as such, were judged in their Representative, being destroyed and necessarily crucified and dying with Him; but not also surrendering His right over these men as His creatures, and therefore not surrendering the right of these creatures of His, but with a view to re-establishing and maintaining it.[25]

In conclusion Barth claims that in the resurrection what God thus does is to make it plain 'that the history of the humiliation of His Son, the history of His way into the far country, is redemption history within universal history; against man, and therefore for him.'[26]

Why? Because on the cross Christ identifies with us in our situation of alienation from God (the 'far country' of the parable of the prodigal son), and the resurrection makes clear that in Christ's cross God is 'against' sinful man to the point of destroying him, but only so that he might be 'for him' as the new and obedient creature Christ's resurrection causes him to be.

The authority of God the Creator

For Barth, then, the resurrection completes the work of the cross and by so doing explains its meaning. As we have also seen, he further holds that it demonstrates the authority of God over human life and death. This is not a major theme in Barth's work, but it is developed in *Church Dogmatics* I/1 in connection with Barth's discussion of 'God as Creator.'

The point that he makes here is that only the one who has power over both life and death is truly 'Lord of our existence' and, as such, the Creator. The one who qualifies for this description is the Father revealed to us in Christ because in the cross and resurrection He demonstrates His Lordship by slaying us in order that He might then give us new life: 'God the Father wills neither our life in itself nor our death in itself. He wills our life in order to lead it through death into eternal life. He wills death in order to lead our life through death to eternal life. He wills this transition of our life through death to eternal life. His kingdom is this new birth.'[27]

---

[25] Ibid. 310–1.
[26] Ibid. 311.
[27] *Church Dogmatics*, vol. I/1, 388–9.

The gift of eternal time in Christ

If the concept of the resurrection as revealing God's authority over life and death is a minor theme in Barth's work, the concept of the resurrection as the means by which God grants us a share in His own eternal time is a major one which occurs in a number of places in Barth's writings. For example in his 1947 work, *Dogmatics in Outline*, Barth declares:

> The third day a new life of Jesus begins; but at the same time on the third day there begins a new *Aeon*, a new shape of the world, after the old world has been completely done away and settled in the death of Jesus Christ. Easter is the breaking in of a new time and world in the existence of the man Jesus, who now begins a new life as the conqueror, as the victorious bearer, as the destroyer of the burden of man's sin, which had been laid upon Him. In this altered existence of His the first community saw not only a supernatural continuation of His previous life, but an entirely new life, that of the exalted Jesus Christ, and simultaneously the beginning of a new *world*.[28]

Barth develops this theme of a new time further in his discussion of 'Jesus, Lord of Time' in *Church Dogmatics* III/2. Building on his basic idea of the 40 days of Easter being a time of revelation he declares that 'The Easter time is simply the time of the revelation of the mystery of the preceding time of the life and death of the man Jesus.'[29] If we ask what the content of this mystery is, Barth's answer is that

> . . . Here, in this creature, in this man, Who had His own time of life and death, and beyond this His time of revelation, God, the Creator and Lord, had already had time before His time, eternal time. It is the time which He took to Himself thus granting it as a gift to the men of all time. It is the time which He willed to have for us in order to inaugurate and establish His covenant. It is the time which is the time of all times because what God does in it is the goal of all creation and therefore of all created time. Since God in His Word had time for us, and at the heart of all other times there was this particular time, the eternal time of God, all other times are now controlled by this time, i.e. dominated, limited and determined by their proximity to it.[30]

---

[28] *Dogmatics in Outline* (London: SCM, 1949), 122.
[29] *Church Dogmatics*, vol. III/2, 455.
[30] Ibid.

What Barth is saying in this very complex statement is that from before the foundation of the world God has willed to give us His own eternal time in Jesus Christ and that the whole purpose of created time is to be the place where this eternal time is given to us. The reason we know that this eternal time has been given to us in Christ is that He is the one in whom eternal time has manifested to us; the one who is the same yesterday, today and forever (Heb. 13:8). And the reason we know this, says Barth, is because 'He has revealed Himself as such, because in the resurrection His appearance has proved to be that of the eternal God.' [31] In other words, by His resurrection from the dead Christ has shown Himself to be the eternal God himself, the one who transcends our finite time limited by death, and as such the one in whom God's eternal time is given to us.

4. The significance of the resurrection for us

If that, according to Barth, is the threefold theological significance of the resurrection how does this impact upon our existence? Barth has three answers here.

First, we need to realise that Jesus' resurrection is the promise of our own. As he puts it in his lectures on the *Heidelberg Catechism:* 'He is the pledge of our own resurrection. We are his members; he is the Head who already exists in living exaltation. Will the Head abandon the members and not draw them after him? He is risen *for us!*'[32]

Second, Barth tells us that the message of the resurrection means that we should have an attitude of joy, of thankfulness and of hope:

> The Easter message tells us that our enemies, sin, the curse and death, are beaten. Ultimately they can no longer start mischief. They still behave as though the game were not decided, the battle not fought; we must still reckon with them, but fundamentally we must still cease to fear them any more. If you have heard the Easter message, you can no longer run around with a tragic face and lead the humourless existence of a man who has no hope. One

---

[31] Ibid. 465.
[32] *Learning Jesus Christ through the Heidelberg Catechism*, 74 (italics his).

thing still holds, and only this thing is really serious, that Jesus is the Victor. A seriousness that would look past this, like Lot's wife, is not *Christian* seriousness. It may be burning behind – and truly it is burning – but we have to look, not at it, but at the other fact, that we are invited and summoned to take seriously the victory of God's glory in this man Jesus and to be joyful in Him. Then we may live in thankfulness and not in fear.[33]

Third, Barth reminds us that we are not called to generate this attitude ourselves. The ability to live as those who are determined by the truth of the resurrection is a result of the power of the resurrection itself at work in us. As Barth puts it: 'Where it is at work the power of the resurrection of Jesus Christ has the irresistible result that man begins to see the light of the promise by and before which he may live, and that he does actually begin to live by this promise which is the form of eternal life itself.' [34]

And the power of the resurrection is effective in us because it is the power of Jesus Christ Himself revealing Himself to us through His Holy Spirit. Having asked the question why the Holy Spirit is the *Holy* Spirit, the one who is able to make us holy people before God, Barth responds:

> He is the Holy Spirit in this supreme sense – holy with a holiness for which there are no analogies – because He is no other than the presence and action of Jesus Christ Himself: His stretched out arm; He Himself in the power of His resurrection, i.e. in the power of His revelation as it begins in and with the power of His resurrection and continues to work from this point. It is by His power that He enables men to see and hear and recognise Him as the Son of Man who in obedience to God went to death for the reconciliation of the world and was exalted in His humiliation as the Son of God, and in Him their own exaltation to be the children of God. It is by His power that He enables them to live in His presence, in attentiveness to His action, in discipleship as those who belong to Him.[35]

In summary, we can say without fear of contradiction that Barth is a theologian with a very clear idea of the nature of the resurrection and of its importance for us. For him, as we have

---

[33] *Dogmatics in Outline*, 123.
[34] *Church Dogmatics*, vol. IV/2, 318.
[35] Ibid. 321–3.

seen, the physical resurrection of Jesus Christ attested to by the empty tomb is the point at which the true identity of Christ is revealed, is the fulfilment of the work of Christ on the cross, is the demonstration of the sovereign power of the creator God and is the point at which the time in which God Himself is present for us is made known to us. It is a summons to us to live in joy, thankfulness and hope, and through the work of the Holy Spirit is the power which enables us to live in this way.

5. The resurrection as 'saga' and 'legend'

All this being the case it would appear that Barth is in fact a conservatives' conservative, a theologian who very firmly rejects the attempts of post-enlightenment liberalism to interpret the resurrection in a non-physical manner or to marginalize its significance. However, as I indicated at the start of this paper, Barth's thought constitutes a challenge not only to liberal theology, but to conservative theology as well. In connection with the resurrection Barth's challenge to conservative thought comes out clearly in the following passage from his lectures on the *Heidelberg Catechism*, which follows on immediately from his criticism of Bultmann's 'demythologization' of the resurrection narratives:

> What is right about the attempt to 'demythologize' the New Testament can only be the clarification of the obvious fact that from a literary historical point of view the Easter message does in fact not have the character of *Historie* [i.e., history which is subject to the investigation and confirmation or refutation of the historical sciences]. What the Easter message reports does not occur in *Historie*. The historian will speak here of saga and legend. If Bultmann wanted only to say that we are concerned here with history (not myth!) in the form of saga and legend, there could be no objection to him. Why should we engage in hair-splitting arguments? But it is not possible to deny the really historical character of the account because it has this form. Why should not saga and legend be a quite appropriate tradition in cases which the form of *Historie* has its natural limitations? The Bible contains innumerable sagas and legends. But it would be false to conclude from this fact that they are not the expression of real happenings. In no case does the Bible intend to present

timeless truths or myths. And so also in this case, it intends to be genuine history (*Geschichte*), but history in a form inaccessible to *Historie*.[36]

There are two points which this passage raises: (1) What does Barth mean by the terms 'saga' and 'legend'; and (2) why does he think that the resurrection, as a real event in the past (*Geschichte*), is not an event susceptible to historical investigation (*Historie*)?

Barth answers the first question for us in a letter to Bishop Theophil Wurm of the Council of the Evangelical Church in Germany in May 1947. In this letter, which discusses Bultmann's theology, Barth explains that the terms 'saga' or 'legend' (which he treats as synonyms) '. . . may relate to real history which took place in time and space but cannot be told 'historically' (i.e. in a form which is demonstrable and illuminating for everybody).' [37]

This explanation moves us on to our second question. If the resurrection really did take place, as Barth believes, in space and time, then why can't it be demonstrated through historical investigation in a way that would convince anyone who approached the subject with an open mind? Generations of conservative apologists, such as Michael Green and Frank Morison mentioned earlier, have argued that it can be demonstrated in this way. Barth says it cannot. Why?

Barth summarizes the reasons why he thinks this way in a long passage in *Church Dogmatics* IV/1 in which he makes four points which for him clinch the issue:

(1). The presence of the angels points us to the fact that the resurrection lies outside the sphere of normal human history: 'We cannot read the Gospels without getting the strong impression that as we pass from the story of the passion to the story of Easter we are led into a historical sphere of a different kind. It is striking that, as at the beginning of the evangelical narratives, mention is made of the appearance and words of angels.' [38]

---

[36] *Learning Jesus Christ through the Heidelberg Catechism*, 76.
[37] B. Jaspert (ed.), *Karl Barth – Rudolf Bultmann: Letters 1922–1966* (Edinburgh: T.&T. Clark, 1982), 144.
[38] *Church Dogmatics*, vol. IV/1, 334.

(2). The resurrection itself is never actually described:

> . . . there is a full account of how Jesus suffered and died, but there is no real account of His resurrection. It is simply indicated by a reference to the sign of the empty tomb. Then it is quietly presupposed in the form of attestations of appearances of the Resurrected. This is all the more striking because the Gospels did fully narrate and describe other resurrections, that of Jairus' daughter (Mt. 19:18–25), that of the young man at Nain (Lk. 7:11–16), and that of Lazarus (Jn. 11) – the latter in a direct and almost plastic way. But here it is not possible to speak of someone superior to Jesus Christ who took Him by the hand and by his word called Him to life from the dead. Here we can only think of the act of God which cannot be described and therefore cannot be narrated, and then of the actual fact that Jesus Himself stood in the midst (Lk. 24:36).[39]

(3). The various resurrection accounts do not add up to a coherent picture of what happened:

> Whether we take the accounts of the resurrection appearances in detail or put them together, they do not give us a concrete and coherent picture, a history of the forty days. Rather we are confronted by obscurities and irreconcilable contradictions, so that we are surprised that in the formation of the canon no one seems to have taken offence at them or tried to assimilate the various accounts of this happening which is so basically important for the New Testament message. There is the further difficulty that Paul not only presupposes and gives in 1 Cor 15: 4–7 another account of what happened, which is different again from the Gospels, but that in 1 Cor. 15:8 (cf. Gal. 1:16) he connects the appearance to himself (obviously the Damascus experience as presented several time in Acts) with the events of those days, although it took place long after the forty days and the *schema* of the forty days is thus strangely broken.[40]

(4). There are no impartial witnesses to what took place:

> . . . the reported appearances according to all the New Testament accounts came only to those who by them were quickened to faith in the crucified Jesus Christ. The appearances cannot, in fact, be separated from the formation and development of the community (or of the original form of the community as the narrower and

---

[39] Ibid.
[40] Ibid. 334–5.

wider circle of the apostles). It was in them that this formation and development took place. None of them is represented as having occurred outside this context.[41]

We shall consider the weight these four points have when we come to evaluate Barth's thought at the end of this paper, but the obvious point which arises from them is how we can know that the resurrection took place if the historical evidence is not such as to provide proof for the independent observer. Barth's answer, which fits in with his general view about the sovereignty of God in revelation, is that Jesus Christ has to make Himself known to us. He Himself is the only one who can come out from the closed door of the cross and make Himself known to us as the risen Lord:

> He and He alone is His own truth. The door cannot be opened from the outside, but only from the inside. It cannot be opened by us, but only by the One who closed it. We can only knock at it, knowing that if it is to be opened it must be from within, by the One who dwells here, and praying that He will open it. Whether it is opened is for Him to decide. It is a matter of His will power and act.[42]

And, as we have seen above, the power which opens the closed door is that of the risen Christ Himself, the one who comes through closed doors, who acts through the Holy Spirit to bring us to faith and make us His disciples.

6. Evaluation

That then is Karl Barth's understanding of the resurrection of Jesus Christ from the dead. What are we to make of his teaching?

The first point that I think needs to be established is that Barth really did believe that the resurrection actually happened. Because of his refusal to say that the resurrection narratives are *Historie* the rumour still circulates that Barth did not believe that the resurrection was a historical event. From the evidence we have looked at in this paper it is clear that this rumour needs

[41] Ibid. 335.
[42] *Church Dogmatics*, vol. IV/2, 297.

to be scotched once and for all. Clearly Barth did believe that the resurrection of Jesus Christ, just as much as His death, was a physical event that took place in our space and time.

This having been said, I think it also has to be said that his assessment of the character of the resurrection narratives is unsatisfactory. The four arguments he gives against seeing the accounts in the Gospels and 1 Corinthians 15 as being 'legend' or 'saga' and not what they prima facie appear to be – historical accounts of what actually happened during the forty days – are simply unpersuasive.

First, the presence of angels cannot by itself mark out an account as non-historical unless one rejects the Biblical idea that angels exist and intervene on occasion in human affairs. Granted this presupposition, which Barth himself accepts,[43] the presence of angels no more marks out an account as non-historical than the presence of human beings within it.

Second, the fact that the resurrection itself is not described, although undoubtedly true, does not call into question the historicity of the accounts of what happened subsequently. The fact that something *is not* described is irrelevant to the question of whether what *is* described actually took place.

Third, although the idea that the resurrection narratives cannot be harmonized into a coherent picture has gained wide currency, it is not an idea we need to accept. In his book *Easter Enigma*, for example, John Wenham has shown very clearly that the accounts of the resurrection can in fact be harmonized in an entirely plausible fashion.[44] This particular emperor has no clothes.

Fourth, the fact that those to whom the risen Christ appeared came to faith is once again irrelevant to the question of whether the accounts of these appearances are historically reliable. If, as the New Testament declares and Barth himself accepts, the character of the appearances was such as to bring about belief in the risen Christ, then a reliable historical account will necessarily reflect this fact. In the nature of the case impartial witnesses are not to be expected.

All this being granted, where I think Barth is on the right track is in pointing us to the fact that whatever the benefits of

---

[43] See his discussion of angels in *Church Dogmatics*, vol. III/3, § 51.
[44] J.W. Wenham, *Easter Enigma* (Exeter: Paternoster, 1984).

attempting to prove the resurrection historically, this is not the strategy that the New Testament itself adopts. Nowhere in the New Testament is there an attempt to 'prove' that the resurrection took place. The fact of the resurrection was not something which the New Testament writers felt they had to prove, it was the certain fact on which their theology was based. Even with regard to 1 Corinthians 15:3–8, which is the place in the New Testament where it can be most plausibly argued that a historical proof of the resurrection is being attempted, I think Barth is correct to say that these verses 'cannot be claimed as an attempt at such a proof.'[45] As Gordon Fee comments: 'Although the enumeration of appearances might suggest otherwise, Paul is not here setting out to prove the resurrection of Jesus. Rather, he is reasserting the commonly held ground from which he will argue against their assertion that there is no resurrection of the dead.'[46]

Moreover, I think Barth is also right in his claim that what enables us to believe in the risen Christ is in the fact of the risen Christ Himself. According to the New Testament witness what brings people to faith is either the direct appearance of the risen Christ Himself or the work of the risen Christ through His Holy Spirit from Pentecost onwards. If we do not follow Barth and the New Testament in recognizing this fact, then three unfortunate consequences follow, which I think we need to avoid:

(a) Faith becomes a human work, an act of our own will and intellectual cleverness, and ceases to be recognized as the divine gift that Ephesians 2:8 declares it to be.

(b) A faith that is dependent on historical proof will always be an uncertain faith since historical investigation can only produce probability and not certainty. Certainty can only be gained through knowledge of the risen Christ Himself.

(c) A faith that was dependent upon historical proof would be a faith that was not open to those lacking the intellectual ability to follow the intricacies of historical scholarship. The faith that is given by the risen Christ, by contrast, is available to all.

---

[45] *Church Dogmatics*, vol. IV/1, 335.
[46] G.D. Fee, *The First Epistle to the Corinthians* (NICNT; Grand Rapids: Eerdmans, 1987), 718.

When we turn to what Barth has to say about the nature and significance of the resurrection here, too, what he has to say is tremendously important and takes us not only to the heart of his own theology, but to the very heart of our faith. There are six main lessons we can learn from him in these areas:

(1). *We have to insist on a physical resurrection and its correlate the empty tomb.* As T.F. Torrance rightly declares:

> If Jesus Christ is risen only in spirit – whatever that means then he is, so to speak, only a ghost with no relevance to men and women of flesh and blood, to human beings who belong to this world of space and time. If Jesus Christ exists no longer as man, then we have little ground for hope in this life, not to speak of the hereafter. It is the risen humanity of Christ that is the very centre of the Christian's hope in life and death.[47]

To put it another way, it is upon Jesus' humanity that His importance for us depends (Heb. 2:14–17), so if that humanity in all its physicality is not raised from the dead, and the tomb is not therefore empty, then the Easter message has no good news for us. To paraphrase Paul in 1 Corinthians 15:14, if Christ has not been raised physically from the dead, then our preaching and our faith are both in vain.

(2). *The real Christ is the risen Christ.* The correct perspective on who Jesus was and is, is provided by the Easter message. It is the risen Christ, the one who died and is alive for evermore and who holds the keys of Death and Hades (Rev. 1:18), who the New Testament proclaims and in whom we are summoned to believe. It is the one who has been exalted and given the name above every name to whom every knee shall bow and whom every tongue shall confess (Phil. 2:9–10). This being the case, the attempt which is still being made in the so-called 'third quest' for the historical Jesus to get back behind Easter in order to discover Jesus' 'true' identity is a complete mistake. As Barth reminds us, it was Easter that revealed who Jesus truly was and is and manifested the eternal glory which He possessed with Father before the world was made (Jn. 17:5). Prior to that His

---

[47] T.F. Torrance, *Karl Barth: Biblical and Evangelical Theologian* (Edinburgh: T.&T. Clark, 1990), 22.

divine glory remained veiled and His true identity was not made fully known.

(3). *The cross is organically connected to the resurrection.* Barth's insistence that the cross and the resurrection together constitute the one great act of God by which we are saved is extremely valuable because it helps us to understand more clearly how Easter provides the answer to our human predicament.

As Tom Smail notes, when we as Christians affirm that 'Jesus saves' we need to be able to answer the obvious rejoinder 'How does He save?' In Smail's words: 'What is it that this one man can do that is so critical and transforming, not just for his contemporaries but for countless numbers of people far removed from him in time and distance? What by dying can one man do that will make possible and actual a new and reconciled relationship to God for all people?' [48]

Barth helps us to answer these questions by pointing us to the teaching of Paul in passages such as Romans 6:1–11, 2 Corinthians 5:14 and Galatians 2:20; and Peter in 1 Peter 2:24, that the cross and resurrection have indeed transformed our fallen state because our old humanity was slain in the death of Christ so that a new humanity might be created when Christ, the second Adam, rose from the dead on the third day. To quote Smail again:

> If we see it like that, then this was a fit work for God in Christ to do on our behalf and in our place. Punishment, confession, repentance are inalienably attached to those who have commited the relevant offences. But Christ entered in love into the sinful situation that was beyond our coping and the fallen nature that was beyond our curing, to execute his transformational justice upon it, so that in the very act in which the old humanity went down to death there was a new creation of a new humanity that was in right relationship to God.[49]

(4). *God is God.* That is to say, the God who is revealed to us in Christ at Easter is the creator God who, because He is creator, has power over both life and death (Rom. 4:17). He can bring life

---

[48] T.A. Smail, 'Can One Man Die for the People' in J. Goldingay (ed.), *Atonement Today* (London: SPCK, 1995), 74.
[49] Smail, 'Can One Man Die for the People', 89–90.

to an end (as on the cross) and then bring new life out of death (as in the resurrection). And because this God is on our side, the fact that He is Lord over both life and death means that neither can separate from His love (Rom. 8:38) and that, as Paul puts it in Romans 14:8–9, 'If we live, we live to the Lord and if we die, we die to the Lord; so then whether we live or whether we die, we are the Lord's. For to this end Christ both died and lived again, that he might be Lord of both the dead and the living.'

(5). *Time is on our side.* If, as Barth rightly says, the resurrection reveals Christ as the one in whom God's eternal time is given to us, the one who is 'the Alpha and Omega, the first and the last, the beginning and the end' (Rev. 22:12), then this means that we do indeed have eternal time. We are not limited to three score years and ten. We have eternity. As Christ Himself said '. . . he who believes in me, though he die yet shall he live, and whoever lives and believes in me shall never die' (Jn. 11:25–26).

(6). *Because these things are so we are not to live as women and men who have no hope.* As Barth says 'we are invited and summoned to take seriously the victory of God's glory in the man Jesus and to be joyful in Him.' Furthermore, not only *should* we live this way, but we *may* live this way because the power of the resurrection, the power of the risen Christ, the power of the Holy Spirit is at work in us. 'If the Spirit of him who raised Jesus from the dead dwells in you, he who raised Christ Jesus from the dead will give life to your mortal bodies also through his Spirit which dwells in you' (Rom. 8:11).

To conclude, what we learn from Karl Barth, and through him from the New Testament itself, is that in the resurrection of Jesus Christ 'God's victory, in man's favour in the person of His Son has already been won.'[50] May we live out that victory in the power of the Spirit of the risen Christ.

---

[50] *Dogmatics in Outline*, 122.

Questions for further study

1. Do you agree that it is vital to affirm the physical nature of the resurrection?

2. Would you be happy to call the resurrection accounts in the New Testament 'legends'?

3. Is Barth right to abandon the attempt to prove the resurrection historically?

4. What is the problem with trying to discover Jesus' identity without starting with the risen Christ?

5. Are you convinced by the idea that the purpose of the death and resurrection of Christ was to destroy our old nature so that a new one might replace it?

6. What might it mean to live as those who take seriously the victory of God in the resurrection of Jesus Christ?

Select Bibliography

Karl Barth, *Church Dogmatics*, Volumes I/1–IV/4 (Edinburgh: T.&T. Clark, 1936–62)

Karl Barth, *Dogmatics in Outline* (London: SCM, 1949)

Karl Barth, *Evangelical Theology* (London/Glasgow: Fontana, 1963)

Bromiley, G.W., *Introduction to the Theology of Karl Barth* (Edinburgh: T.&T. Clark, 1979)

Sykes, S. (ed.), *Karl Barth – Studies of his Theological Methods* (Oxford: OUP, 1979)